The Lincolnshire Wolds

edited by

David Robinson

WIND*gather*
PRESS

Oxford and Oakville

Windgather Press
is an imprint of
Oxbow Books, Oxford

© Lincolnshire County Council, 2009

Lincolnshire County Council has asserted its right under the Copyright, Designs
and Patents Act 1988 to be identified as the copyright holder of this work.

ISBN 978-1-905119-26-4

A CIP record for this book is available from the British Library

This book is available direct from

Oxbow Books, Oxford, UK
(Phone: 01865-241249; Fax: 01865-794449)

and

The David Brown Book Company
PO Box 511, Oakville, CT 06779, USA
(Phone: 860-945-9329; Fax: 860-945-9468)

or from our website

www.oxbowbooks.com

Printed in Singapore by
KHL Printing Co Pte Ltd

Contents

List of Figures

Contributors

David Robinson OBE MSc is a geographer, retired University of Nottingham Department of Adult Education Resident Tutor for Mid-Lincolnshire, former Editor of Lincolnshire Life and The Lincolnshire Poacher, author of 22 books on Lincolnshire landscapes, places and people, President of the Louth Naturalists', Antiquarian and Literary Society and Honorary Secretary of the Lincolnshire Wildlife Trust; he lives in Louth on the edge of the Wolds.

Mark Bennet BA MPhil is Historic Environment Records Officer with Lincolnshire County Council and is Editor of Lincolnshire History and Archaeology, the annual journal of the Society for Lincolnshire History and Archaeology.

Rex Russell BA is retired University of Hull Senior Lecturer in Regional and Local History working in adult education in North Lincolnshire, living at Barton on Humber, and researching and writing particularly on deserted medieval sites and Parliamentary enclosure.

Dr Charles Rawding is Geography PGCE Course Leader at Edge Hill University, Ormskirk, lived for a number of years in the Wolds, and author of 'The Lincolnshire Wolds in the Nineteenth Century'.

Neil Wright DMA is Democratic Services Officer with Lincolnshire County Council, a past Chairman of the Society for Lincolnshire History and Archaeology, with particular interests in the history of Boston and the development of transport in Lincolnshire, author of 'Lincolnshire Towns and Industries 1700–1914' and editor of 'Lincolnshire's Industrial Heritage: A Guide'.

Stewart Squires MBTPI INCB is a consultant town planner, and is still researching and writing on Lincolnshire industrial archaeology.

Terry Hancock is a former librarian with Lincolnshire County Council with a particular interest in the history of the RAF in Lincolnshire and author of 'Bomber County'.

Terry Miller BA is Chaplain for Environmental Issues and Sustainable Development for Churches Together in All Lincolnshire. He is a painter and ceramic artist and has a wide interest in literature and the arts, and is a member of the Lincolnshire Wolds Joint Advisory Committee.

David Hill JP is former Secretary of the Lincolnshire Branch of the National Farmers' Union, with a wide knowledge of changes in farming. He describes himself as a 'Marshman' and worked as a farmer in Lincolnshire for over ten years.

Dr Ted Smith CBE MA was founding Honorary Secretary (in 1948) and is now President of the Lincolnshire Wildlife Trust. Former University of Nottingham Department of Adult Education Resident Tutor for South-East Lindsey. Author of 'Trustees for Nature: A Memoir'.

Penny Baker BA has successfully managed a range of regeneration and tourism initiatives throughout the East Midlands over the last nineteen years. Since 1998 she has been Chief Executive of Lincolnshire Tourism, which is regarded as one of the UK's leading destination marketing partnerships.

Ray Taylor was formerly an officer with Lincolnshire County Council and later with the Heritage Lottery Fund.

Steve Jack BSc PGDip DMS has over fifteen years experience in environmental and community projects. He has been Manager of the Lincolnshire Wolds Countryside Service since 2002, working on behalf of the Lincolnshire Wolds Joint Advisory Committee and supported by a dedicated AONB team based at the Navigation Warehouse, in Louth.

Acknowledgements

....

This book was first conceived in 2001 as part of the Lincolnshire Wolds Interpretation Project, where thanks are due to Ruth Fish (then Countryside Agency), Steve Catney (then Lincolnshire County Council), Graham Barrow, project officer, and more recently to Jon Watson, Lincolnshire County Council Environment Team Leader. A book about the making of the landscapes of the Wolds and their changing land use, how they have been seen through literature and art, and the designation and management of the Area of Outstanding Natural Beauty was seen as a vital element in raising awareness and understanding.

As both commissioning editor and contributor, I am grateful to all the other authors for their collaboration and patience, to Richard Purslow (formerly Windgather Press) for guidance in planning the content, to Mark Bennet for advice on presentation. I owe a particular debt to staff of the Lincolnshire Wolds Countryside Service: to Manager Steve Jack, to Project Officer Louise Niekirk for identifying and collating illustrations from their collections to supplement those provided by authors, and especially to Administrative and Technical Assistant Jenny Evans who completed the text in digital format and whose work creating disks was critical to the preparation of the book.

David Robinson, Editor

A contribution towards the production and publishing of this book was made from Lincolnshire County Council's Lincolnshire Wolds Interpretation Project 1999–2002. This project was funded by the European Agriculture Grants and Guarantees Fund through MAFF (now Defra); Lincolnshire Economic Action Partnership (LEAP), the Countryside Agency (now incorporated in Natural England) and Lincolnshire County Council.

Foreword

I was born in 1950, in the Lincolnshire Wolds and I am therefore I suppose, umbilically connected to this land and this landscape. Whether it is this, or something else buried deep inside me that gives me my innate and deep passion for the Wolds I don't know. I only know it exists.

Over the last fifty-nine years the Wolds, like other parts of the English countryside have undergone a radical change in the way they look and are worked, for let us never forget, this is a living working landscape that has been and continues to be, subservient to the will of man. The change in farming practices, the need for more and more housing, better and bigger roads, additional and more extensive utility supplies and distribution and an ever increasing population all make demands and impact upon our landscape. As do the natural threat of global warming and let us not forgot the changes wrought by Dutch elm disease. But all of these can be managed if we care enough about our natural environment to be sensitive in the way we use it, manage it and care for it. To do that we need to understand it and the impact it has upon our lives, our sense of place and wellbeing and its value beyond its capacity to produce food.

I hope when you read this book you will gain a better understanding of the history of the Lincolnshire Wolds and the people who have lived and worked in them. I hope, for those of you who have never visited them, you will be inspired to come and see for yourself what makes them special, feel the sense of peace and solitude as you gaze from the Caistor High Street across to Lincoln Cathedral or immerse yourself in the gentle folds and valleys that are so characteristic of this countryside.

We have it in our power to ensure that this special landscape (recognised by its designation as an Area of Outstanding Natural Beauty in 1973) is protected and enhanced for the good and enjoyment of this and future generations. We can all play a part, from the landowner to the visitor. If we are sensitive to the needs of the land, its flora and fauna, and those who live and work here, it will survive and prosper.

I hope you enjoy this book but more than that, I hope it will awaken or rekindle a passion for the Lincolnshire Wolds, a very special little bit of England.

Bernard Theobald
Chairman of the Lincolnshire Wolds
Area of Outstanding Natural Beauty Joint Advisory Committee

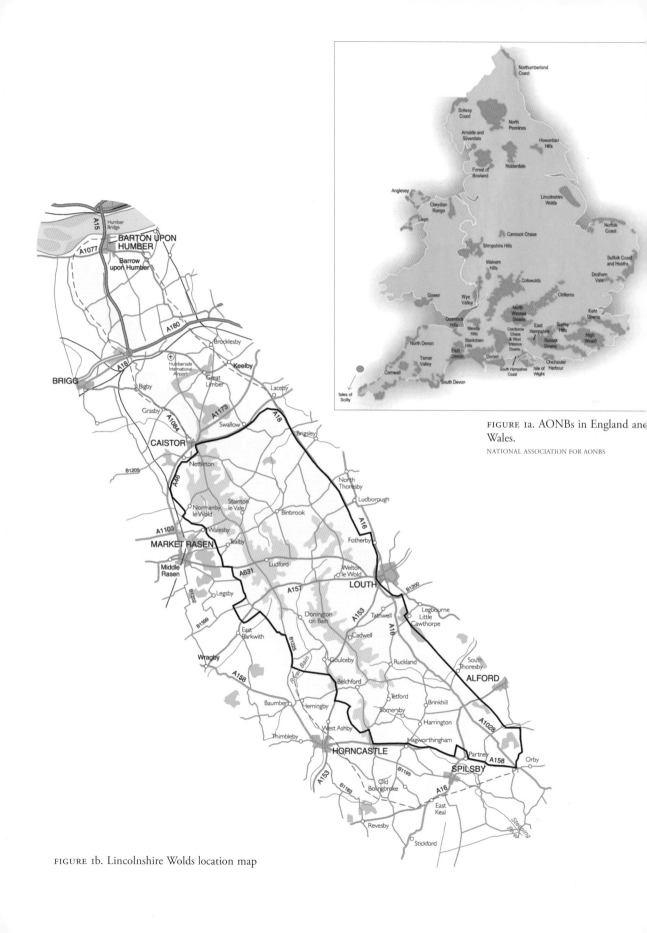

FIGURE 1a. AONBs in England and Wales.

NATIONAL ASSOCIATION FOR AONBS

FIGURE 1b. Lincolnshire Wolds location map

CHAPTER ONE

The Shaping of the Wolds

David Robinson

The Lincolnshire Wolds form the highest ground in eastern England between Yorkshire and Kent, rising to 168m (550ft) near Normanby le Wold. Often referred to as the Chalk Wolds, in fact the White Chalk is only a cap to the hills, nowhere more than about 100 m (300ft) thick. Below it is a series of relatively thin sandstones, ironstones and clays, and below them a more resistant sandstone, all on a thick base of clay.

Due to the gentle eastward dip of the rocks which make up the Wolds, there is a prominent west-facing escarpment, with Chalk on the crest, relatively smooth from South Ferriby to Caistor. From there south to about Sixhills the scarp is deeply fretted by the Nettleton and Usselby Becks and the River Rase. North of Donington on Bain the scarp is broken by the River Bain, unusual in that it flows south parallel to the rock formation. From Stenigot to Candlesby the scarp is again prominent, with coombe features, but faces south-west overlooking the valley of the River Lymn where the river flows on clay surrounded by a wide ledge of sandstone, with another ridge beyond.

By contrast the eastern edge of the Wolds is truncated in a nearly straight line from Barton on Humber to Candlesby: this was a line of chalk sea cliffs rising to about 60m (200ft). Those once spectacular white cliffs of the Wolds are now masked by deposits left by glaciers, but the slope is still significant as at Ashby Hill and Miles Cross Hill (above Alford) for example.

The tops of the Wolds are generally plateau-like, inclined gently to the east. North of a line from Caistor to Laceby the presence of dry valleys produces a smooth rolling landscape. To the south of that line the tops are divided by the extensive headwater systems of the Waithe Beck, the River Lud and the Calceby Beck/Great Eau. The eastern part is also marked by some eighty short, steep-sided and open-ended valleys, the classic example of which is Hubbard's Hills near Louth.

To understand the evolution of these landscapes we need first to look at the underlying rocks, how the original hills were formed, and the influence of rivers and ice upon them. The oldest rocks are the dark grey shaley clays, the **Kimmeridge Clay**, laid down in a relatively deep stagnant ocean 150 to 160 million years ago towards the end of the Jurassic era. Fossils to be found include bivalve shells (usually crushed), ammonites and vertebrae of the marine reptile Ichthyosaur. The clays outcrop as inliers in the valleys of the River Lymn and its tributaries, Sow Dale, and the Rivers Bain and Waring. An unusual and

FIGURE 2. The north-western escarpment with Searby nestling at the foot.
DAVID ROBINSON

localised feature within the clays is the 6m (20ft) thick **Elsham Sandstone**, of clear quartz sand with some lime-cemented masses rich in fossils including ammonites, formed by a flush of fast-flowing water. It occurs on the lower slopes of the escarpment above the village of Elsham and on the Wrawby Spur. Some layers of the Kimmeridge Clay are rich in organic material which stimulated a fruitless search for coal at Benniworth Haven. The Clay Vale to the west of the Wolds escarpment is partly floored by Kimmeridge Clay (now known there as the Ancholme Group), and extends southwards under the Fens.

The main foundation rock of the Wolds is the **Spilsby Sandstone** which marks the transition from the Jurassic to the Cretaceous era, around 140 million years ago. The bottom metre (3ft) of dark sand is rich in glauconite, a green silicate of iron, phosphatic nodules and fragments of ammonites eroded from the top layers of the Kimmeridge Clay when the sea had become very shallow. Succeeding beds vary in thickness from 6 to 21m (20–30ft), and vary vertically and laterally from fine gravel through course sands to fine sand, with glauconite present throughout. So some beds are greenish and hardened with calcareous cement, while others are iron-stained. Both types of beds have fossil bivalves, and the cemented layer at Tetford yielded belemnites and ammonites of the same species as have been found in similar beds in Russia and Siberia – evidence of the extent of the shallow seas in which the sands were laid down.

The top 1.2m (4ft) of the Spilsby Sandstone are ferruginous and pass into the **Claxby Ironstone** where the iron is in the form of ooliths. The rock is brown with a clay matrix and iron ooliths, and some beds are particularly fossiliferous with large oyster and pecten (scallop) shells. The maximum thickness is at Claxby and Nettleton, thinning south-east where there are non-ferruginous interbedded clays – the **Hundleby Clay**.

As the sea deepened, deposits changed to dark grey clays, the **Lower Tealby Clay**, followed, as the water became clearer and warmer, by the creamy, cemented and fossiliferous **Tealby Limestone** with some shaley beds and oolitic iron before reverting to clay again – the **Upper Tealby Clay** varying from dark grey to buff in colour and yielding small pieces of fossilised wood. Being tougher than the clays below and above, the Tealby Limestone forms a prominent ledge on the scarp slope between Audleby and Donington. As a localised rock, it gives an indication of the varying conditions on the sea bed about 130 million years ago.

Oolitic iron reappears in the **Fulletby** or **Roach Beds**, the lowest and uppermost being virtually an ironstone, while the middle beds are tough and sandy forming the Roach Stone. This also determines a ledge feature at the south end of the Wolds, as at Skendleby, Grebby, Scremby and Candlesby, and caps isolated hills round the Lymn valley, noticeably at Hoe Hill near Fulletby and Dalby Hill.

Above the Fulletby Beds is 3m (10ft) of the black and grey **Sutterby Marl**, with some belemnite and ammonite fossils. Then follows 9m (30ft) of the khaki-coloured **Carstone**, ranging upwards from fine sand to course grit with tiny highly polished pebbles, laid down over a considerable period of time. The deposit is without fossils. In the Wolds the Carstone easily crumbles, yet little more than 30 miles away in north Norfolk it is tough and well cemented.

The sequence of Lower Cretaceous deposits – sandstone, ironstone, clay, limestone, clay, ironstone, sandstone – indicates changes from shallow to deeper water, then shallow again, consistent with a nearby shoreline moving further away and then getting closer again. This is supported by the presence of polished pebbles in both sandstones, they being the result of wind sand-blasting under

FIGURE 3. The southern internal escarpment at Belchford where ploughing reveals the colour sequence of Carstone, Red Chalk and White Chalk.
DAVID ROBINSON

desert conditions on the nearby land. The other factor which has affected the Wolds landscapes today is that the Lower Cretaceous sequence of rocks thins northwards, had been subject to erosion north from Audleby, and is completely missing and overstepped by the White Chalk of the Upper Cretaceous at South Ferriby. Hence the simple scarp slope of chalk over clay in the north contrasts with the complicated landscapes of limestones, clays, ironstones and sandstones of the southern Wolds.

The Upper Cretaceous period, from about 100 million to 65 million years ago, saw an extensive transgression of the sea over all except the, then, highest part of the British Isles. Initially the warm sea was probably quite shallow resulting in the condensed deposit of the **Red Chalk**, the thin (1.5–3m/5–10ft) outcrop of which provides vivid splashes of colour on steep hillsides. It varies from a dark red marl at the base to pink hard nodules at the top, and contains abundant fossils of small belemnites, bivalve 'lampshells' and the occasional small ammonite. The method of formation is not yet fully understood, but the colour is probably due to red lateritic mud being washed into the sea from nearby low-lying land with a tropical climate.

The change to the succeeding **White Chalk** is abrupt and marked by a thin layer of fossilised branching sponges (the Sponge Bed) indicating a marked climate change accompanied by deepening of the sea up to 150 fathoms (275m). The White Chalk accumulated slowly as a pure chemically precipitated calcareous ooze at the rate of about 0.3m (1ft) every 30,000 years. The maximum deposit was over 300m (1,000ft) but the greatest thickness left in the Wolds is about 90m (300ft) near Louth, much of the higher zones having been removed by later erosion. The White Chalk may owe its purity to the arid climate of the low-lying land away to the north-west with little surface drainage. In the

FIGURE 4. The open-ended glacial meltwater spillway cut through a spur of the chalk at Swaby.
DAVID ROBINSON

Lower Chalk (now known as the Ferriby Formation) there are pink bands and a particularly hard grey bed, the 'Totternhoe Stone'. The change to the Middle Chalk (the Welton Formation) is marked by a thin marl band, the Plenus Marl, thought to represent volcanic ash from a short-lived eruptive period on the land area. The Upper Chalk (Burnham Formation) is only found in the northern Wolds. Fossils to be found in the White Chalk include sponges, sea urchins, bivalve shells, ammonites (some the diameter of a car wheel) and fish teeth. Beyond the clear-cut eastern edge of the Wolds the Chalk dips away under the Marsh and is continuous under the Wash to Norfolk, and extends north across faults of the Humber valley to the Yorkshire Wolds.

A feature of the White Chalk is the presence of grey flints. Excepting the Ferriby Formation, they occur as nodules of various shapes in the Welton Formation and in flat tabular or lenticular masses up to 0.5m (18ins) thick and extending over many square miles in the Burnham Formation. There are also hollow flints (potstones) and occasionally large conical Paramoudras; the largest, 2.3m (7ft 6ins) high and 1m (3ft 4ins) in diameter at the top, was found in the now infilled Ashby Hill chalk quarry. Flint is almost pure silica and formed as a gel from sponges, from silica squeezed out of solution in sea water, by periodic variation of the seabed ooze, or from silica-rich water percolating down from a later land surface.

At the beginning of the Tertiary era about 65 million years ago the tropical sea retreated, Britain was upwarped and the Chalk emerged as a gentle dome so that weathering and rivers could begin to remove successive layers. Then between 25 and 12 million years ago came the last great mountain building activity which created the Alps. Lincolnshire felt only a minor outer ripple, subsidence in the North Sea accentuating the easterly dip of the rocks of the Wolds, and the development of the Audleby Monocline, a one-sided fold with a downward displacement to the north of up to 90m (300ft). This accounts for the change of direction of the west escarpment of the Wolds between Bigby and Audleby, and in part for the lower topography to the north. Associated step-faulting along the Humber gap separated the Yorkshire Wolds from the Lincolnshire Wolds. In the south there is a north-west to south-east fault along the line of the Driby and Claxby valleys, and the big gap between the Wolds and the chalk cliff at Hunstanton, now largely filled by the Wash, perhaps owes its origin to downwarping of the Chalk.

Land levels were higher than now, and the main drainage pattern of independent Humber, Lincoln, Ancaster and Wash rivers was established. The last 10 million years of the Tertiary saw final removal of the extensive White Chalk cover to the west, and Lincolnshire was virtually the same level as the sea, having been worn down to a peneplain. On the Wolds this is represented by the concordant plateau surfaces at 150 to 130m (500–400ft), along the line of the Bluestone Heath Road and the High Street for example, making them among the oldest land surfaces in Lincolnshire. As the sea gradually receded there were periods of stillstand when sea-level was constant, leaving what have been claimed to be former marine platforms as bevels on ridges and spurs in the Wolds at 130 to 115m (420–380ft) and 67 to 55m (220–180ft). At each stage of lowering sea-level the clays to the west of the Wolds were quickly worn down and the escarpment pattern began to emerge. Streams would also have been initiated on the dip-slope of the Wolds.

By about a million years ago the sea had retreated to some 40 miles off the present Lincolnshire coast, and the Wolds north of Hainton and the Lower Cretaceous rocks on the base of Spilsby Sandstone in the south-west Wolds had taken basic shape. The escarpment was being cut back and fretted by spring-head sapping, that is erosion of the weaker rocks and collapse of harder rocks above. The middle River Bain, Scamblesby Beck and River Waring etched valleys between the main chalk scarp and the subsidiary Lower Cretaceous ridge to the west, separated by spurs at Colley, Flint and Park Hills on that ridge. On the east, down the dip-slope and through another prolonged period of stillstand when sea-level was some 26m (70ft) lower than now, waves again cut their way into the land, removing lower reaches of valleys and truncating spurs to create vertical chalk cliffs which gradually retreated to near the present eastern margin of the Wolds.

The **Pleistocene** was marked by periods of increasing cold, interspersed with times of temperate or near sub-tropical conditions, with related movements of sea-level. During an early, warmer, higher sea-level phase, marine erosion probably produced the Burnham Surface at 67 to 55m (220–180ft). A later phase, probably about 500,000 years ago could have produced the Brocklesby Park Surface at 40 to 24m (130–80ft). Of earlier ice advances, which on Norfolk evidence may have been over half a million years ago, there is no trace on the Wolds, but a later glaciation nearer 250,000 years ago (formerly known as the Wolstonian) left behind the Calcethorpe Till at Welton le Wold (and the Welton Till), and in the Bain valley and central Lincolnshire. Originating from Scotland and Northern England, this ice scraped and ground its way roughly north to south across the Wolds, smoothing and lowering the northern escarpment, incorporating soil, chalk and flints into the base of the ice, and fracturing and

FIGURE 5. Hoe Hill, Fulletby: an outlier of Lower Cretaceous rocks capped by the Roachstone.
DAVID ROBINSON

FIGURE 6. The distinctive Red Chalk in the scarp face of Red Hill nature reserve above Goulceby.
DAVID ROBINSON

cambering the scarp edges in the south of the Wolds. During a pause in the ice advance meltwaters poured into the upper Bain valley and laid down the Biscathorpe Gravels, and then the ice itself pushed through and enlarged the gap, and buried the gravels. Other gravels, incorporating earlier temperate fauna (elephant, deer and horse) and Palaeolithic (Early Stone Age) flint tools, which had accumulated in the Welton le Wold valley were also covered by till as the ice advanced over them.

When the climate finally ameliorated the ice melted, revealing the basal material and dumping its load of rock debris as boulder-clay or till. This is the intensely-chalky boulder-clay (the Calcethorpe Till) still left in patches to the north-west of Louth (the Kelstern 'plateau'), on the south-west Wolds capping the Lower Cretaceous ridge, spreading into the Clay Vale to the west and beyond Horncastle under the Fens. As glaciers melted decaying masses of ice remained in the mid-Lincolnshire Clay Vale where it had been thickest. This forced the ice-free River Bain to take a route southwards cutting into the Calcethorpe Till but able only to receive left bank tributaries, primarily the Scamblesby beck and River Waring. Hence the high ground on the west of the valley, followed by the 'ramper' from Horncastle to Baumber and the High Street from there, marks approximately the ice-edge position at that stage.

The later Ipswichian Interglacial lasted about 45,000 years from around 120,000 to some 75,000 years ago. Sea-level rose to between 3 and 5m above the present level as evidenced by the buried beaches at Sewerby near Bridlington in Yorkshire and Hunstanton in Norfolk. On the eastern side of the Wolds wave action eroded the chalk cliffs further westward until, north of Louth, they were up to 90m (300ft) high and with a beach of flints at the base, similar to those on the coasts of Kent and Sussex today. The sea also cliffed the Spilsby Sandstone

FIGURE 7. A bed of tabular flint in the Upper Chalk at West Ravendale.
DAVID ROBINSON

outcrop at the southern end of the Wolds, best seen at West Keal, and to a lesser extent the chalky boulder-clay from East Kirkby to Mareham le Fen.

Further incision of dendritic Wolds valleys took place at this time, the headwaters of stream systems cutting back towards the western crest of the hills. The Freshney and Waithe Beck systems cut down through the Chalk to the lowest (Ferriby) beds and in places to the Carstone and Roach Formation, with headwaters near Thoresway, Stainton le Vale and Kirmond le Mire. The Wolds crest between there and the increasingly incised valleys of the Nettleton and Usselby Becks and the River Rase, which exposed most of the Lower Cretaceous rock including the Claxby Ironstone, became very narrow where the High Street skirts the heads of the east-facing valleys north of Bully Hill. The Lud system was also developed further with the Welton Beck cutting into the older glacial deposits at Welton le Wold, was the middle Lymn in the southern sandstone Wolds; but the most spectacular incisions were those of the Calceby Beck system. There the headwaters cut back by vigorous spring-head sapping down into the Tealby Clays, developing steep-headed coombes, as at Oxcombe where the Wolds crest is at its narrowest at barely a hundred metres.

Perhaps the events most influential in moulding the Wolds landscapes, particularly in the east and south-east, were the two glaciations of the **Devensian**. The first reached its maximum some 45,000 to 40,000 years ago and the second around 22,000 to 20,000 years ago. Ice had accumulated yet again and spread out from Scotland and Northern England, with a large lobe of glacier-like ice squeezed southwards along the east coast by an ice sheet spreading across the North Sea basin from Scandinavia. The ice pushed through the gap between the Yorkshire and Lincolnshire Wolds extending as far as Winteringham and to Horkstow in the Ancholme valley. It over-rode

FIGURE 8. The upper part of the interglacial sea cliff on the eastern edge of the Wolds exposed in the Fir Hill Quarry nature reserve near Little Cawthorpe.
DAVID ROBINSON

the chalk cliffs of the northern Wolds to 60m (200ft) near Burnham, pushed into the Barnetby gap to Kirmington, and edged towards Limber, Swallow and Wold Newton. Further south it jammed against the Kelstern plateau at over 110m (370ft), penetrated the Welton and Hallington valleys, over-rode most of the chalk ridge up to 90m (300ft) as far as Ketsby, South Ormsby, Driby and Ulceby, pushed over the Candlesby spur to Skendleby and Partney, and extended as far as Stickney and Boston and across to Norfolk thus closing the Wash gap. The overall effect was to block the eastern flowing drainage of a large part of eastern England, impounding Lakes Humber and Fenland linked through the Lincoln gap. The Wolds, therefore, became in effect an 'island' under arctic conditions, with permafrost and tundra vegetation, between the ice to the east and a lake periodically frozen over to the west.

Frost shattered exposed rocks in the winter, not least at the heads of valleys, and summer snow-melt carried away the debris. The Nettleton and Usselby Becks and the River Rase tumbled into the impounded lake, and the River Bain delivered a large outwash deltaic fan of flinty gravels into the shallows of Lake Fenland around Tattershall. These gravels contain the remains of mammoth, woolly rhinoceros and deer which had been trapped on the tundra island and probably died of starvation.

On the east, however, the outflow of Wolds streams was blocked by ice and the summer snow-melt had to develop alternative escape routes. From Wold

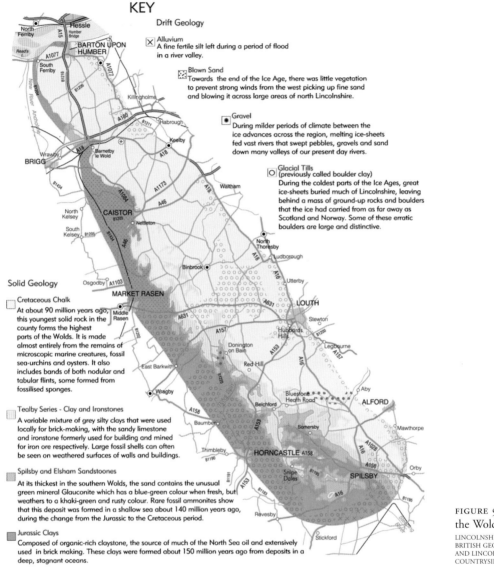

KEY

Drift Geology

☒ **Alluvium**
A fine fertile silt left during a period of flood in a river valley.

▨ **Blown Sand**
Towards the end of the Ice Age, there was little vegetation to prevent strong winds from the west picking up fine sand and blowing it across large areas of north Lincolnshire.

◉ **Gravel**
During milder periods of climate between the ice advances across the region, melting ice-sheets fed vast rivers that swept pebbles, gravels and sand down many valleys of our present day rivers.

◯ **Glacial Tills**
(previously called boulder clay)
During the coldest parts of the Ice Ages, great ice-sheets buried much of Lincolnshire, leaving behind a mass of ground-up rocks and boulders that the ice had carried from as far away as Scotland and Norway. Some of these erratic boulders are large and distinctive.

Solid Geology

▢ **Cretaceous Chalk**
At about 90 million years ago, this youngest solid rock in the county forms the highest parts of the Wolds. It is made almost entirely from the remains of microscopic marine creatures, fossil sea-urchins and oysters. It also includes bands of both nodular and tabular flints, some formed from fossilised sponges.

▢ **Tealby Series - Clay and Ironstones**
A variable mixture of grey silty clays that were used locally for brick-making, with the sandy limestone and ironstone formerly used for building and mined for iron ore respectively. Large fossil shells can often be seen on weathered surfaces of walls and buildings.

▢ **Spilsby and Elsham Sandstoones**
At its thickest in the southern Wolds, the sand contains the unusual green mineral Glauconite which has a blue-green colour when fresh, but weathers to a khaki-green and rusty colour. Rare fossil ammonites show that this deposit was formed in a shallow sea about 140 million years ago, during the change from the Jurassic to the Cretaceous period.

▢ **Jurassic Clays**
Composed of organic-rich claystone, the source of much of the North Sea oil and extensively used in brick making. These clays were formed about 150 million years ago from deposits in a deep, stagnant oceans.

FIGURE 9. The rocks of the Wolds.

LINCOLNSHIRE TOURISM, BRITISH GEOLOGICAL SURVEY AND LINCOLNSHIRE WOLDS COUNTRYSIDE SERVICE

Newton northwards those waters carved sinuous 'in and out' (that is open-ended) channels along the thin, feathered edge of the stagnant ice, across valley divides and eventually found their way west through the Barnetby gap, dropping their load of gravel into the lake. The beach of clattered flints and Palaeolithic (Old Stone Age) tools at Kirmington at the east end of the Barnetby gap is best explained as a former and lower interglacial beach which had been pushed up to that height by the advancing ice edge.

South from the Kelstern plateau the waters cut a complex series of shorter channels eventually feeding into a smaller proglacial lake in the lower Lymn valley, and then escaping west along the ice edge and into Lake Fenland near

West Keal leaving a train of outwash gravels. Good examples of the channel system can be seen at Haugham and at Deepdale Firs across the interfluve south-west of Burwell. The ice front at South Ormsby obstructed the wide valley on Lower Cretaceous rocks at Tetford, meltwater formed a shallow lake which then made an escape south by cutting the dramatic New England gorge through the Spilsby Sandstone. This became a permanent route for the Tetford waters between Salmonby and Somersby (Tennyson's Brook). In some places along the ice front warm summers melted it back in stages, resulting in a series of shallow parallel channels, as to the east of Deepdale Firs and between Ketsby and South Ormsby.

The incursion of ice to near Welton le Wold, where the Devensian Till rests on the much earlier Welton Till and even earlier gravels in the Welton valley, make the area critical to understanding the sequence of glaciation in eastern England. The privately owned gravels area is a Site of Special Scientific Interest and the Devensian Till site to the east is a Lincolnshire Wildlife Trust Regionally Important Geological Site (both are former quarries).

There then followed a period of some millennia when there was no ice on the Wolds, and when the Wash gap and then the Humber gap became free of ice the drainage system returned to normal activity, except where there had been permanent stream diversion as at New England. The new raw rock-sided meltwater channels were modified to a smoother profile: one of the best examples in the north Wolds is the Ash Holt spillway crossed by the minor road from Swallow to Croxby Pond. Absence of permafrost allowed exploitation of joining in the chalk and in at least two of the channels, near Swallow and near Walmsgate, small sink holes or swallets developed. As Lake Humber drained away, and while conditions were still relatively cold, sands from the dry sandstone shore of the former lake in Nottinghamshire were blown east across unvegetated ground.

During the final onset of cold, about 22,000 years ago, the ice only impinged on the eastern Wolds from Brocklesby to Aby, over-riding the till left from the previous period of glaciation and the then partly-masked cliff, and again penetrating the Waithe Beck, Welton and Hallington valleys, but not extending as far as the previous glaciation. It did however again obstruct Humber drainage to create a second, lower Lake Humber. As the ice passed over the chalk it planed off a smooth surface, as was revealed by roadworks at the junction of Grimsby Road and St Mary's Lane in Louth. East flowing streams again had to carve new escape channels. Where ice pushed into east-facing valleys and stagnated, thinning of the ice left blocks of dead ice, resulting again in a complex series of channels and of outwash sands and gravels laid down in cold conditions. Being younger, these channels are fresher, more steep-sided and more dramatic, as around Hatcliffe.

Just north of Irby meltwater escaped first northwards through Irby Dales and Washingdales, and later east through Rush Hill. At Hatcliffe where the lobe of ice filled the original valley, meltwaters cut the Deepdale and Flint Hill spillways,

FIGURE 10. Outcrop of the grey/green beds of Spilsby Sandstone, the main building stone for churches in southern Wolds, such as nearby Somersby.

BOTH DAVID ROBINSON

FIGURE 8. Relocating the Bluestone glacial erratic from Northumberland outside Louth Museum.
DAVID ROBINSON

effecting a permanent diversion of the stream. South-east of Hatcliffe another escape route can be followed along minor roads: from The Valley south of Wold Newton, north through the village and past Petterhills and East Ravendale, where there were temporary small lakes with silty clay deposits, then north-west through the West Ravendale and Round Hill spillways – both excellent examples of 'in and out' valleys. West of Louth are the two-stage Welton Vale and South Elkington spillways, and of course Hubbard's Hills (described elsewhere). South of Louth is the twisting spillway channel, now just within the west boundary of Burwell Wood, from which waters passed into the Valley Farm channel just north of Swaby, where there is another classic double-bend spillway which became a permanent stream diversion – the Swaby Valley.

Beyond the ice limit the south-east trending and relatively fresh-sided valleys at Haugh, Well Vale and Skendleby Psalter were stripped of any earlier glacial deposits by summer snow-melt during that last glaciation. Ploughing of the thin chalk soils of the Wolds today shows up rill patterns of darker soils where snow-melt from the interfluves slid into main valleys.

Both during and between the last two glaciations minor features of the Wolds landscape developed the shapes we see today. On the Nettleton scarp there were landslips where the unstable Tealby Series outcropped, the harder rocks squeezing out the clays below. On the inner scarp to the south, Gaumer Hill near Scamblesby and the smaller Rasin Hill above Belchford became separated from the scarp as Roachstone-capped outliers. Above Tetford and at Langton by Spilsby smooth coombes were formed by patches of melting snow slipping down the scarp face. On the east side of the Wolds, at the junction of boulder-clay and chalk, springs emerged at Welbeck Hill, Little Cawthorpe, Belleau and Claxby by Willoughby.

The rock fragments within the glacial tills reveal where the ice, which so influenced the eastern Wolds landscapes, originated. There are gneisses and schists from the Scottish Highlands, granites from the Grampians, basalts, volcanic ashes and red sandstones from Central Scotland, Millstone Grit and coral and grey limestones (on which ice scratches are best seen) from the northern Pennines, carbonaceous siltstones from the Durham coalfield, calcareous gritstone from the North Yorkshire Moors (there is a billiard-table-size slab at Welton le Wold), fossiliferous mudstones from the north Yorkshire coast, chalk and flints (of all shapes and sizes) from the Yorkshire Wolds, and the distinctive igneous rhomb porphyry from southern Norway. But perhaps the most iconic are the 'bluestones' – large chunks of dolerite (a basalt) plucked from the Whin Sill on the coast of Northumberland, frozen into the moving glacier, transported to Lincolnshire and dumped when the ice finally melted. The best example of a bluestone is on display outside Louth Museum. There is no connection with the ancient trackway the Bluestone Heath Road along the crest of the Wolds. The boulder-laden Devensian ice never reached that far. The road probably took its name from the blue flowers on the grassy track.

Ice finally decayed and disappeared from the eastern Wolds some 20,000 to 18,000 years ago, and from Britain about 10,000 years ago. Devensian time gave way to the Flandrian, a period when fluvial and marine deposits over the Outmarsh displaced the shoreline some ten miles from the Wolds. Drying out of the second Lake Humber again exposed lacustrine and outwash materials to blowing, and sands were banked against the northern scarp of the Wolds from Grasby to Nettleton, with scarp-foot spreads southwards as far as North Willingham. There are also a few patches of such sands on the Wolds near Caistor. The treeless tundra of the Wolds gradually changed towards temperate vegetation patterns related to the varying soils derived from underlying rocks, glacial deposits and slopes. It was still the Stone Age, and hunter-gatherer man was back in occupation.

I am grateful to Emeritus Professor Allan Straw for help in preparing this chapter.

Hubbard's Hills

Towards the end of the Ice Age, around 20,000 years ago, glaciers from Scotland, northern England and Scandinavia invaded the eastern Wolds for the last time. Despite the steep edge of the hills, steeper than now, the pressure behind the advancing ice squeezed lobes of it into the Welton and Hallington valleys, blocking the eastward flow of their streams. As the climate began to get less cold, what was left of the decaying ice and all its deposits of boulder clay (till) in the Hallington valley impeded the immense quantities of spring and summer melt flowing into the valley from the Wolds and ponded them back into an extensive and deep lake.

The lake water found an escape route northwards across the chalk ridge to cascade as a waterfall into the Welton valley. As the waterfall eroded back it created the Hubbard's Hills gorge. Such was the force and erosive power of the water that it took perhaps little more than 250 to 300 years to slice right through the ridge of jointed and frost-shattered chalk and drain the lake.

At the north end of the gorge another decaying block of ice in the Welton valley diverted the river east, which then turned south to escape by tunnelling under the ice and then flowing in a temporary channel between the decaying edge of the glacier and the steep edge of the Wolds.

As the glaciers finally melted away from east Lincolnshire around 12,000 years ago they left behind extensive deposits of hummocky boulder clay and patches of outwash sands and gravels, which is now the Middle Marsh. Similar deposits in the lower Hallington valley ensured the permanent diversion of the river through the gorge, which then developed a natural winding course as weathering and soil slip softened the original near vertical sides.

Crowd at the opening celebration on 1 August 1907.
DAVID ROBINSON COLLECTION

In post-glacial times the slopes colonised with downland grasses and scrub. No woodland was recorded in the Domesday Survey in the eleventh century, when the valley was in Hallington parish, the boundary with Louth running along the top of the eastern side. By the second half of the eighteenth century Hubbard's Hills was in the ownership of the Chaplin family and treated as part of a sporting estate. The name Hubbard's Hills was firmly established by the 1820s, named after a tenant farmer, as was Fisher's Hill on the west side, and Dog Kennel Farm was built for the South Wold Hunt hounds. Pastures in the valley were divided by hedges and the steep valley sides planted with conifers. Landscape engravings made in the 1840s show the use of footpaths through the valley and particularly up the eastern side to the path along the parish boundary.

The Waterworks were built in 1872 to the design of Louth architect James Fowler, and five years later the lake in the valley was constructed to provide a head of water for the watermill just downstream. With the Bank Holiday Act of 1871 and opening of the Bardney to Louth railway in 1876, Hubbard's Hills became a popular destination for excursions during Lincoln's Foundry Trip Week in July, and a favourite place for rambles by Louth people. A little booklet 'How the Lud cut through Hubbard's Hills' was available and by the early twentieth century at least thirty different picture postcards were on sale.

The Chaplin lands were sold in 1905, and two years later the trustees of Auguste Pahud, a Swiss teacher at King Edward VI Boys' Grammar School in Louth who had committed suicide in 1902, bought Hubbard's Hills to perpetuate the memory of his late wife. Some 35 acres were purchased for £2,025, together with a further 8½ acres, part of which was planted with ash, sycamore, larch, Scots pine and spruce. Following the building of rustic bridges and shelters and a memorial fountain, Hubbard's Hills was formally handed over to the Borough as a country park for the town on 1 August 1907.

A model of the making of Hubbard's Hills can be seen in Louth Museum.

David Robinson

CHAPTER TWO

The Wolds before AD 1000

Mark Bennet

Archaeological survey in the Wolds has been relatively limited until recently. The Ordnance Survey collected archaeological information to revise the six-inch maps of the county from the late 1920s through their correspondent C. W. Phillips. He published a summary of Lincolnshire's archaeology in 1933–34. In this he was reliant on a number of local archaeologists, including the professional museum curator Harold Dudley at Scunthorpe, amateur archaeologist Harry Preston of Grantham, and Ethel Rudkin who had a wealth of knowledge about the county. There was one independent museum in the Wolds, at Louth, founded in 1910 by the Louth Naturalists', Antiquarian and Literary Society. It holds a small number of local Prehistoric, Anglo-Saxon and Medieval finds.

Amateur archaeologists continued to make useful contributions to the archaeological record of the Wolds. In the Lymn valley Geoffrey Taylor collected information and carried out several small-scale excavations on land that he and his brother farmed near Salmonby after the Second World War, and William Bee has been systematically field-walking and recording flint scatters. Other amateur archaeologists have carried out field-work in their parishes, for example J. Clark and Mrs J. Mostyn Lewis at Claxby and Normanby and D. Everatt at Thoresway.

More formal archaeological surveys were conducted in the 1980s. One of these, carried out by the Trust for Lincolnshire Archaeology, targeted the Bain valley, and there was a transect by the University of Sheffield across the northern Wolds. This latter survey included some work on long barrow sites and was complemented by analysis of aerial photographs by Dilwyn Jones. The wealth of cropmark and earthwork evidence from aerial photography is particularly valuable for understanding the archaeology of the Wolds.

More recent survey work has been on the southern sandstone edge, and on a large estate in the northern Wolds that included earthworks in woodland that are probably surviving Prehistoric linear ditched boundaries.

The results of surveys and discoveries help to create a picture of the human development that affected the landscape of the Wolds. The earliest peoples who ranged across the Wolds lived in the Palaeolithic (Old Stone Age) from about 525,000 years ago to the final melting of ice sheets from the Wolds some 18,000 years ago. Although much of the evidence for early Palaeolithic occupation was damaged or destroyed by later glaciations, significant finds have been made in the Wolds.

At Welton le Wold, a former gravel quarry revealed hand-axes associated with mammalian remains in gravels beneath later glacial deposits. The finds, made in the 1970s, are not in primary context but are in good condition and have not been moved far. The importance of the site lies in having a clear stratigraphic relationship between hand-axes and dateable layers. The presence of hand-axes shows that early humans did exploit the Wolds before the last glaciation.

Other lower Palaeolithic finds of worked flints were made in a quarry at Kirmington, also beneath glacial deposits, on a layer of coarse shingle. The site was a storm beach in a valley through the former chalk sea cliff on the eastern edge of the Wolds when sea level was much higher than today.

Evidence for upper Palaeolithic activity is confined to the Lymn valley, where a flint knife from Fulletby is a rare piece of evidence of human recolonisation of the Wolds after the Ice Age. In the late glacial period the environment was similar to the tundra landscapes of northern Canada today, with few trees and plant life dominated by sedges and mosses. Human activity was seasonal with small bands of hunters pursuing reindeer or horse during the summer. As sub-arctic conditions began to ameliorate, vegetation began to re-establish with grasses and dwarf shrubs. As the Palaeolithic merged into the Mesolithic (Middle Stone Age) and average temperatures rose, trees began to appear.

The Mesolithic was a time of hunter-gatherers, small groups of people, probably linked by family ties, moving from place to place as the seasons and resources of plants and animals dictated. Evidence for Mesolithic activity is usually found in transitional zones between landscape types, and depends on finds of worked flint and other stone. There have been few early Mesolithic finds, from 10,000 to 8,000 years ago, and most comprise only one or two flints,

5cm

FIGURE 12. A Lower Palaeolithic hand-axe found at Salmonbury.
M. BENNET

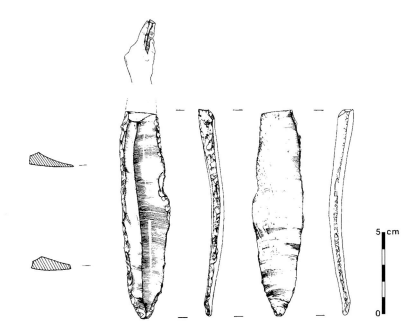

FIGURE 13. An Upper
Palaeolithic flint knife
from Fulletby. Drawn by
R. Cook.

COURTESY OF SOCIETY FOR
LINCOLNSHIRE HISTORY
AND ARCHAEOLOGY

for example at Salmonby and Walesby. A site in Claxby parish at the foot of the Wolds scarp is interpreted as a possible campsite.

Later Mesolithic finds are relatively more numerous with a noticeable concentration on the wind-blown sands on the western edge of the Wolds. It may be that game was attracted to natural clearings in woodland and people may have created small clearings to attract the animals.

There are Mesolithic flint scatters in the Lymn valley around Tetford and on the southern edge of the Wolds overlooking low-lying land to the south. Five sites in the Bain Valley were all found at the head of small tributary streams. At any one time during this period, the population of Lincolnshire may have been no more than 70 to 140 people. Foraging areas involved exploitation of the landscapes adjacent to the Wolds and beyond to the coast for fish, crustacea and shell fish.

From about 4,000 BC the later hunter-gatherers began to grow crops and husband livestock. It marks the change from the Mesolithic to the Neolithic (New Stone Age), and it was during the Neolithic that forest clearance began on the Wolds. There is evidence from excavations of the Giant's Hill long barrow at Skendleby for clearance of deciduous oak and hazel woodland perhaps as early as 3,500 BC. Analysis of pollen and mollusc remains from soil in the ditches of long barrows indicates a grassland environment in the immediate vicinity. There is also pollen evidence for cereal crops in plots or small fields, while animal bones suggest that cattle, pigs and sheep were raised in the later Neolithic. Bones of auroch, a species of wild cattle, were found at Ash Hill and Giant's Hill long barrows.

Evidence for Neolithic activity in the Wolds is dominated by the surviving long barrows. Recent work by Dilwyn Jones identified 56 sites of long barrows or mortuary enclosures in the Wolds, far more than in any other part of Lincolnshire. They show a marked clustering on the east of the Wolds, in the valleys of the Waithe Beck and the Great Eau, and also in Fordington Bottom that flows into the River Steeping, suggesting areas where early Neolithic people lived.

On the other hand, Neolithic axe-heads made from flint and from other stone have a more widespread distribution, and have been taken as evidence for widespread forest clearance and settlement. Their distribution shows two distinct clusters on the Wolds: one in and around the parish of Thoresway and the other in the Lymn valley, although this distribution is possibly due in part to the selective activities of field-workers. In the Lymn Valley the finds of axe-heads and parts of axe-heads over more than seventy years have been made by a number of individuals. Thus this cluster is not the result of the activity of only one or two field-workers. The axes have both a functional and a symbolic importance and more emphasis has recently been placed on their ritual deposition. Perhaps the Lymn valley was a prime location for the ritual deposition of axe-heads, in contrast to those valleys to the east where long barrows are found.

FIGURE 14.
Reconstruction of Skendleby long barrow.
D. HOPKINS

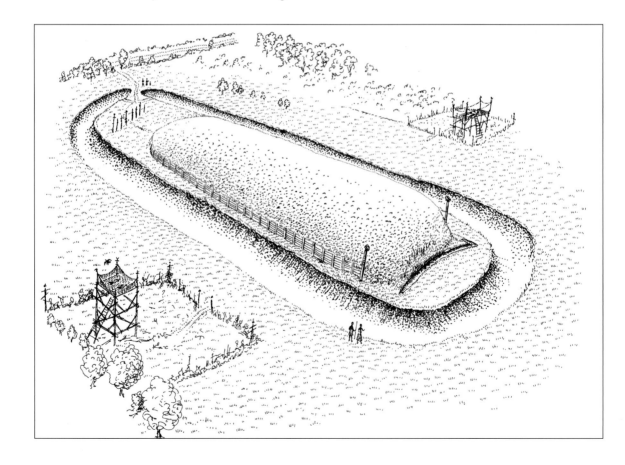

It was during the Neolithic that people began the practice of building large ritual monuments in the landscape to mark places significant to them. It may be that this continued much earlier traditions of recognising certain places as sacred. Long barrows are the most numerous of those ritual elements of this Neolithic landscape. There is evidence from the Giant's Hill long barrow at Skendleby that an earlier sepulchral monument stood on the site before the mound of the barrow was built.

The human remains found in excavated long barrows are usually disarticulated and are not complete skeletons. The bodies of the dead were defleshed, probably through excarnation, laying out bodies in the open until the soft tissues have disappeared. The bones of the dead had a special and continued significance to the communities that used the monuments. Bones are found redeposited in different locations within long barrows as well as being ritually redeposited in other places that were also important to local communities. The relatively large number of long barrow monuments in the Wolds is an indication of the ritual significance of these uplands.

Other ritual monuments of the Neolithic and Bronze Ages include a henge (a circular ceremonial site defined by a bank and ditch) in the Bain valley near West Ashby with a diameter of 25 metres and a circle of pits outside the ditch which may well have held wooden posts. Smaller henge-like monuments have been identified at Stainton le Vale in the valley of the Waithe Beck and at Calceby in the valley of the Great Eau.

A short cursus-type monument, a long narrow enclosure with two parallel ditches, has been identified at Thorganby and linear pit-defined monuments at Stenigot in the valley of the Bain and Bag Enderby in the Lymn valley. These monuments are a double alignment of paired pits which may have held timber posts at regular widely spaced intervals. It is suggested that they acted as a focus for sepulchral-ritual ceremonies.

FIGURE 15. A general shot of Giant's Hill Neolithic long barrow under excavation in the early 1930s.
COURTESY OF LINCOLNSHIRE COUNTY COUNCIL

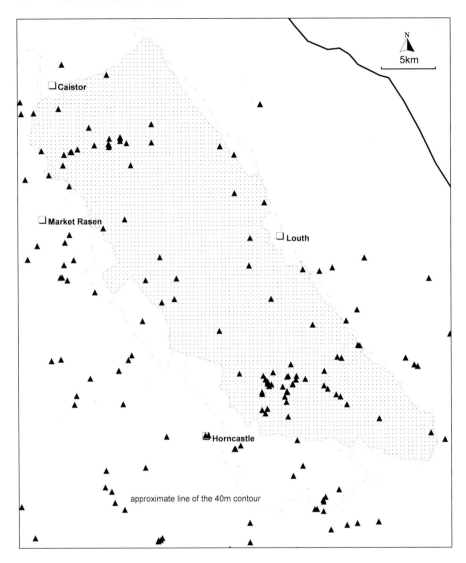

FIGURE 16. The distribution of Neolithic axe-heads in the Wolds. The shaded area is the Wolds AONB. Data from the Lincolnshire Historic Environment Record of Lincolnshire County Council.

There is evidence that long barrow sites continued to be used in the later Neolithic although not necessarily for the burial of human bones. At Giant's Hill long barrow the ditches were refilled and later pottery was found in the ditches. The evidence from snail remains and charcoal in the ditches of the barrow show that the adjacent land had reverted to dense woodland of yew and ash with some oak, and shrub including hazel and blackthorn.

Settlement sites with evidence of permanent or semi-permanent huts, occupation debris or evidence for fields, from the Neolithic and Bronze Age have always been difficult to find and are rare in Britain as a whole. However, work on a reservoir in Donington on Bain revealed tentative evidence for an early field system with small rectangular plots and access trackways. Also, in the Bain valley, excavations of the West Ashby barrow found early Bronze Age

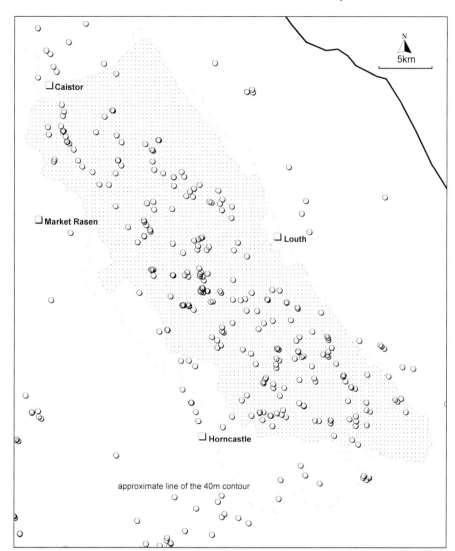

FIGURE 17. The
distribution of Bronze
Age barrows showing
the large numbers in
the Wolds with fewer
found in the surrounding
landscapes. Most of
these barrows have
been recognised from
cropmarks visible in
aerial photography. The
shaded area is the Wolds
AONB. Data from the
Lincolnshire Historic
Environment Record
of Lincolnshire County
Council.

Within the map: Caistor, Market Rasen, Louth, Horncastle, approximate line of the 40m contour, N, 5km

flint work and pottery in the make up of the mound as well as similar flint work during field-walking in the vicinity. The conclusion was that the barrow lay close to a settlement. In 1986 a gas pipeline trench cut through a number of features in Swallow and domestic material was recovered, suggesting the remains of a Bronze Age settlement.

The monuments that would have dominated the Wolds landscape in the Bronze Age were the round barrows. These earthwork mounds survived for many centuries, and in 1852 it was still possible to write of 'a chain of tumuli or barrows stretching from the Humber to the interior of the country'. Evidence of many more survive as cropmarks, indicating ring ditches, seen on aerial photographs. Over 350 barrows and possible round barrows are now recorded in the Wolds. Good examples of easily seen round barrows are along the Caistor

FIGURE 18. Bully Hill Bronze Age round barrow. One of several in the Wolds that survive as earthwork mounds. This one stands beside Caistor High Street in Kirmond le Mire parish.
COURTESY OF LINCOLNSHIRE COUNTY COUNCIL

High Street, near Tealby and Ludford for example, and the group of seven at Bully Hills near Tathwell.

Bronze Age barrows were often placed near to earlier monuments. Those landscapes were often in fairly open grassland and it is possible that, in parts of the Wolds, barrows were used for marking territorial grazing rights. There is evidence from excavations at Giant's Hill long barrow at Skendleby for further extensive woodland clearance at the end of the Neolithic and early in the Bronze Age. This was followed by some cultivation before the area became grassland in the later Bronze Age and into the Iron Age.

The discovery of how to smelt and work iron did not have a major impact on the cultural and social life of Prehistoric people in the short term. The settlement pattern and economies of the late Bronze Age and early Iron Age are similar. Late Bronze Age tools have been found on the Wolds, notably a number of bronze socketed axe-heads. Ritual deposits of bronzes, however, have only been found in rivers and fen edge locations just off the Wolds.

There are a number of cropmark sites of enclosures in the Wolds, plotted from aerial photographs, several with late Iron Age and Romano-British artefacts found on them. Enclosure ditches at Kirmond le Mire investigated in 1991 were found to date from the late Bronze Age from pottery found there. Earthwork survivals have been found on the northern Wolds, and would have been highly visible in an open landscape. There is a hill fort on the Wolds, on the north side of the Kirmington gap near Croxton, known as Yarborough Camp. It is not certainly Iron Age although finds of Roman pottery suggest the date of occupation. A large enclosure at Swinhope Hill near Binbrook may perhaps date from the late Bronze Age to early Iron Age. Cropmarks reveal small ring ditches within the enclosure which have been interpreted as evidence for round houses.

A bird's eye view of the Wolds a generation or so after the Roman Conquest would not have revealed very much difference in the general pattern of the landscape to that of the pre-Roman late Iron Age. The small fort near Croxton covered the northern gap through the hills, and newly metalled Roman roads led to saltmaking sites on the coast, but the majority of small farmsteads would have looked much the same. Most of the archaeological evidence for the start of the Roman period in the Wolds points towards continuity rather than dramatic change.

Small farmsteads were scattered across all parts of the Wolds, and there are widespread finds of Romano-British pottery. Odd finds of quern stones indicate some arable farming with cereal crops for domestic use. Some of the farmsteads have elements of curvilinear ditches which indicate an Iron Age origin. Others have rectilinear enclosures, several with Romano-British pottery.

Excavations at Barnetby le Wold revealed a late Iron Age farmstead that continued to be occupied into the Roman period. There was no evidence for any profound change as a result of Roman political control; traditional circular wooden buildings were constructed well into the Roman period. There was little Roman pottery being used on the site, even as late as the second century AD. It may be that the impact of Roman material culture on rural Iron Age people in the Wolds was limited for several generations after the Roman invasion. It has been suggested that this community deliberately chose to ignore the Roman artefacts and other symbols of Roman cultural dominance as a protest against the changes that the Romans brought. It was only in the later second century that changes in the development of the farmstead took place when small corn-driers were built, and then larger stone ones in the mid third century. These indicate that arable crops were being grown, with environmental evidence for wheat, and that the community was prepared to invest in stone buildings. At Stenigot Reservoir near Donington on Bain part of another farmstead was excavated which demonstrated there was arable cultivation of wheat, barley and oats, together with evidence of features used to control stock animals, and finds of bones of cattle, pigs, sheep, horse and dog.

Larger Roman sites are easier to recognise and where they include evidence of mosaics, hypocaust tiles (under-floor heating), painted plaster-work or domestic stone buildings they are commonly called 'villas'. These high-status farms were a feature of the later Roman period and there are several on the Wolds including Worlaby, Kirmond le Mire and Walesby. The Lymn valley was an important area of quite dense Roman settlement, aerial photographic evidence revealing a landscape of small 'villas' and associated enclosures.

There are a number of large (up to thirty hectares) settlement sites in Roman Lincolnshire, some of which have been called 'small towns'. Although the cropmark evidence for these sites can be very extensive, their whole area was not necessarily occupied all at the same time. There are several small town

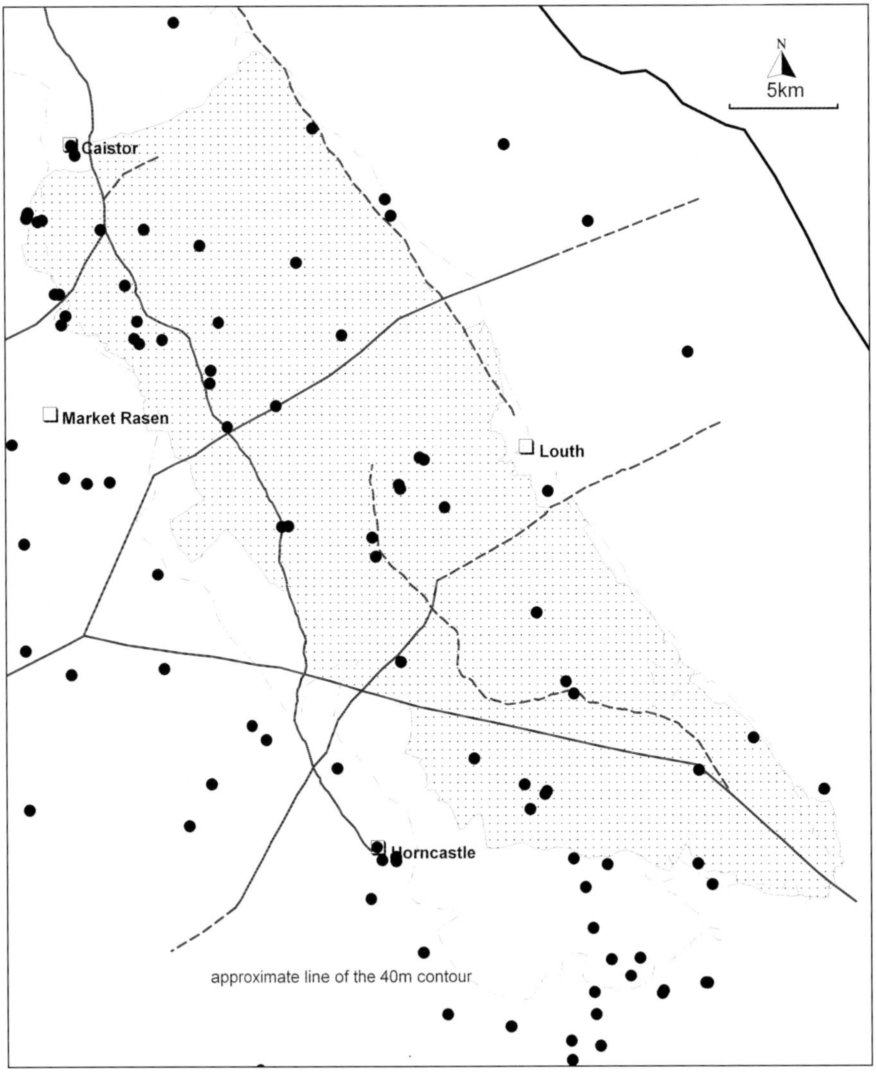

FIGURE 19. The distribution of Roman settlement in the Wolds. The roads and routeways shown include both known Roman roads and routes that are presumed to have been in use during the Roman period. The shaded area is the Wolds AONB. Data from the Lincolnshire Historic Environment Record of Lincolnshire County Council and the North-East Lincolnshire Sites and Monuments Record of North-East Lincolnshire Council.

settlements in the Wolds all apparently developed from late Iron Age proto-urban sites. These open, undefended settlements seem to have functioned as economic, political and social centres during the Iron Age and into the Roman period. Sites are known at Kirmington, Ludford, Horncastle, Ulceby Cross and Spilsby with a possible site at South Ferriby cliff. Settlements have also been recorded at Nettleton Top adjacent to the Caistor High Street, and from cropmark evidence at Aswardby in the Lymn valley. Recent excavation at Nettleton Top revealed substantive remains of late Iron Age and early Roman occupation. Earlier finds had indicated the presence of a shrine or temple complex, with similar evidence at Kirmington.

There were two small later Roman forts in the Wolds at Horncastle and at Caistor. Both had stone walls and date to the late third century or later. The

Horncastle walls enclosed a rectangular area of two hectares, and the Caistor enclosure fortified an area of three and a half hectares. At Horncastle the fortifications of Spilsby Sandstone were built at the confluence of the rivers Bain and Waring and were outside the area of the earlier late Iron Age and Romano-British settlement to the south. At Caistor the defences follow the lie of the land, and although there is evidence for Roman settlement, there is little evidence for any substantial earlier Iron Age occupation. It seems that these fortifications were part of a defensive system for the east coast of Britain. Horncastle and Caistor probably acted as bases for units of mobile light troops that could react quickly to any barbarian raiders.

There is a traditional picture of the end of Roman rule coming in AD 410, with Angles and Saxons then arriving from the continent and taking over large areas of the countryside. In fact, the collapse of the Roman economy and the end of the Romanized way of life was probably much more gradual and would have happened at different rates across the country. The Anglo-Saxons arrived in Lincolnshire within a couple of generations of the end of Roman rule, although there is some evidence for a limited Germanic presence during the fourth century. The collapse of the Roman economic system led to changes in the landscape as the larger high-status Roman farms declined and disappeared, with a return to small farmsteads and minor settlements.

It is the burial grounds of the pagan Anglo-Saxons that provide much information on the period from the fifth to the seventh centuries. There are several of the larger cremation cemeteries in the Wolds, most notably at South Elkington near Louth and at Hall Hill, West Keal. Cremated remains were buried in urns and date to the early part of the Anglo-Saxon period in the fifth and sixth centuries. Two hundred and ninety burials were plotted at South Elkington, with only about a quarter of the cemetery excavated (in 1946–47) and the scatter of pottery from cemetery urns at Hall Hill covered about two acres. Cremation urns from South Elkington are exhibited in Louth Museum. The cemetery at Elsham, excavated in 1975–76 found, over 600 urns. There is the possibility of a further cremation cemetery near Wold Newton where over twenty urns were discovered during gravel extraction in 1828.

These large cemeteries probably serviced a wide area, with communities bringing their dead some distance to be buried. The rituals associated with the burial of cinerary urns were important in early Anglo-Saxon funerary ceremonials. For settlers who took part in the rites, the ceremonies served to emphasise their group identity. These cemeteries were special places in the landscape for the families that used them and it is not surprising to find them in prominent locations. Hall Hill overlooks the northern fens and the Stickney ridge with its evidence for early Anglo-Saxon settlement, and Acthorpe Top at South Elkington looks out across the Lindsey marshes towards the sea. The site of the Elsham cemetery has a view from the western edge of the Wolds towards and across the valley of the River Ancholme, as well as views to the east.

Later inhumation cemeteries are more numerous and generally smaller

FIGURE 20. An Anglo-Saxon cremation urn from the cemetery at South Elkington watercolour, probably by C. M. Pearson (one of the volunteers who worked on the site).
COURTESY OF LINCOLNSHIRE COUNTY COUNCIL

than cremation cemeteries. They rarely have more than a hundred graves, and probably served individual settlements or small groups of settlements. They were also on high ground, with a line of them along the eastern edge of the Wolds at Brocklesby, Keelby, Riby, Laceby and Welbeck Hill.

One of the more interesting burials in the Wolds is at Asgarby, discovered in 1915, where grave goods indicate it to be of a warrior with a sword, shield and a variety of rich accoutrements. It dates to the seventh century and may be that of an aristocrat, perhaps even a prince of the kingdom of Lindsey, a small independent Anglo-Saxon kingdom for at least part of the sixth and seventh centuries.

When pagan inhumation cemeteries ceased to be used, from about the late seventh century, Anglo-Saxon archaeological evidence is much sparser. Christian burials without grave goods became the norm. Pottery scatters in the south of the Wolds indicate some settlement in East and West Keal and Toynton St Peter, together with some evidence of continued occupation of Roman sites into the middle Saxon period.

Excavated settlement sites on the Wolds have found sunken-featured buildings consisting of a pit with a post-hole at each end. One at Riby had farming compounds for livestock, where evidence from bones suggested cattle with lesser numbers of sheep were kept. There was also some evidence for arable crops and for textile production using wool or flax. Occupation of the site lasted until the mid ninth century. A similar settlement, at Nettleton Top, also grew arable crops, mostly barley.

High-status centres in the Wolds included Horncastle and Caistor which were royal sokes or estates, and there were early monasteries at Partney and possibly Louth. Two of the three markets in the Wolds recorded in the Domesday Book of 1086 were at Louth and Partney, perhaps associated with the monastic centres, and may have originated in the middle Anglo-Saxon period. Recent analysis of finds has stressed the wealth of Lindsey during the period leading up to the Scandinavian take-over, where sites close to Barton Street along the eastern edge of the Wolds have yielded middle Anglo-Saxon coins and other metalwork together with pottery imported from the continent. These suggest that the natural resources of the Wolds were being exploited and commercial links established with other parts of Britain and with the continent.

Evidence for woodland on the Wolds during the Anglo-Saxon period is limited. The Domesday Book recorded little woodland and it would seem that only sparse woodland remained by 1086. However, there is some evidence for a royal estate centre at Waltham within a wooded area. This is based on the place-name 'Waltham', an early settlement name, deriving from '*weald*' or '*wald*' meaning woodland, high forest land, and '*-ham*' meaning an estate or administrative centre. It was perhaps associated with an estate on the Wolds that was regarded as forest even though it was less wooded than the royal forests in the south of England. The place-name Limber derives from the Old English name for the lime tree, a native species and indicative of ancient woodland. If this is evidence for woodland in Waltham, it is early and middle Anglo-Saxon and not recorded in the later Anglo-Saxon period.

Scandinavian settlers probably arrived in Lincolnshire from 877 when the great Viking army split up and parts of Mercia were shared out among the warriors. It seems that the large estates were fragmented into smaller holdings, many of which later formed the manors recorded in the Domesday Book. At the same time there was a movement towards more nucleated settlements and the core of many present day villages began at this time. The new landowners needed to emphasise their status and one way they did this was by founding churches on their land. By usurping ancient rights, notably the right of burial from the episcopal minsters, these new churches served the lordship of their founder and became the centres of new, small parishes.

Recent work on Anglo-Saxon stone sculpture has shed new light on the formation of parishes in Lincolnshire. Most of the stone sculptural pieces found are the remains of the monuments of an elite. It is suggested that they were the monuments of the founders of new churches, buried in newly established graveyards. Because it is possible to date the sculpture, the foundation of parochial graveyards perhaps began in the early to mid tenth century. The particular style of these monuments in Lindsey from about 950 may indicate a connection with the re-establishment of the Bishop's authority after Wessex re-conquered Lindsey in 942. In the Wolds, therefore, the creation of parishes occurred during the mid to late tenth century as the local magnates founded parochial churches on their land and sought the support of the new Bishop.

The landscape of the Wolds today has been formed by the activities of mankind since the last Ice Age. The inhabitants of the Wolds during each period of pre-history and history have left evidence of their passing. Even today there are landscape elements in the Wolds that were created by the activities of people who lived thousands of years ago. Seeking to understand how and why a landscape has been formed will help us to manage, protect and enjoy that landscape.

CHAPTER THREE

Medieval Desertion

Rex Russell

The sites of as many as 220 deserted villages have been identified within Lincolnshire; of which 71 sites are on the Wolds. Located by extensive aerial photography, map evidence, detailed field-work and by documentary evidence, many of the sites are hard to recognize on the ground today. Much destruction has taken place since the 1940s through bulldozing and ploughing to extend the arable acreage: especially in the 1960s and 1970s. Most of the destroyed sites have been recorded from the air, for example Burnham (in the west of Thornton Curtis parish), Swinhope (north of Binbrook), Ketsby and a hamlet site within Kirmond le Mire parish. Several excellent sites still clearly visible include North Ormsby (north of Louth), best seen when the setting sun reveals a road, boundary banks limiting individual farm building sites, and (less obviously) house sites, all of which can be viewed from the public road; Calceby, with the ruins of its church, can be seen from the Bluestone Heath Road; and Beesby from the road from Binbrook to North Thoresby (the site of its church is prominent in the paddock just east of the farmhouse). For the majority of deserted medieval village sites one needs the consent of the farmer on whose land they lie to make a visit.

A selection of known sites is clearly indicated on Ordnance Survey maps: O.S. 1:50,000 Landranger sheet 113 gives the sites of (for example) Acthorpe, Beesby, North Ormsby and West Wykeham; and O.S. 1:25,000 Explorer sheet 282 gives more and also shows the plans of North Cadeby, Wyham and North Ormsby.

Medieval churches still stand on several deserted village sites and visits to these underlie the fact of desertion. A little north of Louth one can visit both Wyham church (All Saints) made redundant in 1982 and now in private hands; the chancel may be eleventh century – see the herring-bone masonry on the south side. Hawerby (St Margaret) was made redundant in 1978; it is also now in private hands but can be seen in its churchyard. This was partly restored in the seventeenth century with stone from the demolished church of Beesby; the livings of Hawerby and Beesby were amalgamated *c.*1450. From the ruins of Calceby church the Norman doorway is thought to have been re-used in South Ormsby church. Other churches which are visible from public roads are on the deserted sites of Farforth, Driby (converted to a private house) and Worlaby (near Tetford) where the church was only built in *c.*1880.

Very little expert excavation has been undertaken on these sites. Good

FIGURE 21. Site of the deserted village of North Ormsby showing rectangular cottage plots.
DAVID ROBINSON

reports on such work are in print for Burnham (in Thornton Curtis parish) where very substantial remains of the church were discovered together with a stone image of its patron saint, St Lawrence. Although Goltho lies off the Wolds near Wragby, the report of extensive excavation in the 1970s tells much about medieval occupation. The periods of desertion for many sites have been carefully estimated by the dating of medieval and early post-medieval pottery and iron-work found on them soon after ploughing and bulldozing. Metal-work such as keys, locks, ox shoes, horse shoes and spurs can all be dated.

The reasons for desertion are, at present, known for a small minority of sites. 'At Oxcombe on the Wolds a loud protest from the parson in 1633 tells us that the lords of the town had turned the fields into pastures and sheepwalks; at Withcall, south of Louth, the lord was preparing in 1681 to change the Westfield from crop-growing to the keeping of sheep; at Hainton and Sixhills the Heneage family carried out some enclosure in Elizabeth's and James' reign...' (Joan Thirsk, *English Peasant Farming*).

Not far from Oxcombe are the deserted sites of Farforth, Maidenwell, Ketsby, Worlaby, Walmsgate and Calceby. It may well be that these desertions were for the same reason as at Oxcombe – landowners and farmers changing production from the less profitable cereal crop to much more profitable sheep-farming/wool. Why did such change go on despite Parliament passing Acts against depopulation? Between 1489 and 1597 no fewer than eleven such Acts was passed, but deliberate depopulation continued. They continued because the local major families who should have enforced the Acts chose to ignore them, for personal profit. 'Where monks showed an example [of depopulation], the gentry of the fifteenth century onwards followed. In 1631, the list of 'depopulators' who had been dealt with by the Council included the names of Hussey, Ayscough, Whichcote, Carre, Wray, Rossiter, Tyrwhitt and Bussey – the best-known families in the county' (Maurice Barley, *Lincolnshire and the Fens*).

The preambles of two of the Acts against depopulation help to understand some Wold village desertion:

1515. An Act Avoiding Pulling Down of Towns
'The King … calling to his most blessed remembrance that where great inconveniences be and daily increase by dislocation, pulling down, and destruction of houses and towns within this realm, and laying to pasture lands which customable have been manured and occupied with tillage and husbandry, whereby idleness [unemployment] doth increase, for where in some one town 200 persons, men and women and children, and their ancestors out of time or mind, were daily occupied and lived by sowing corn … breeding of cattle, and other increase necessary for man's sustenance, and now the said persons and their progenies be minished and decreased, whereby the husbandry … is greatly decayed, Churches destroyed, the service of God withdrawn, Christian people there buried not prayed for, … market towns brought to great ruin and decay … to the high displeasure of God and against his laws and to the subversion of the common weal of this realm …'

1533–5. An Act Concerning Farms and Sheep
'Forasmuch as … sundry [persons] of the King's subjects of this realm, to whom God of his goodness hath disposed great plenty and abundance … now of lat … have daily … invented ways and means how they might accumulate and gather together into few hands … great multitude of farms … and in especial sheep, putting such lands as they can get to pasture and not to tillage, whereby they have not only pulled down churches and towns and enhanced the old rates of their rents … by reason whereof a marvellous multitude … of the people of this realm, be not able to provide meat, drink and clothes necessary for themselves, their wives and children, but be so discouraged with misery and poverty that they fall daily to theft, robbery … or pitifully die for hunger and cold …'

The Black Death of 1349–51, which carried off about a third of the population of Lincolnshire, was the first of a series of visitations of the plague. No village was completely depopulated by the first blow, but the effect of recurrences was cumulative, particularly on the poorer Wolds soils where productivity was diminished. The poll tax record for 1377 shows that Maidenwell had 25 adults (some 50 inhabitants in all), but by 1429 there were fewer than ten families, and in the mid-century the village was relieved of about half its tax quota. It never recovered.

A result of shrinking congregations was that empty or near-empty parishes were amalgamated with their neighbour. In 1397 East and West Wykeham were united with Ludford Magna because there was no incumbent and the parishioners had died or left on account of the pestilence. At Calcethorpe, where the village street and cottage platforms can still be seen, the church was down by 1450, and adjacent Kelstern, where the church remains, is very much a shrunken village.

A third reason for disappearance of a medieval village, but not the population, was emparkment. An example is South Ormsby where the present road from Tetford diverts round the park created when the house was built in 1752–55, with estate cottages to replace the few remaining mud and stud dwellings, the sites of which are now under the grassy park.

FIGURE 22. Ruin of St Andrew's church, Calceby – all that remains of the deserted village.
DAVID ROBINSON

The Lincolnshire Rising

At Evensong in St James's parish church, Louth on Sunday 1 October 1536, the Vicar, Revd Thomas Kendall, warned parishioners that the King's Commissioners, having already closed down Louth Park Abbey, would be in the area to dissolve Legbourne Priory and might also seize the church jewels, plate and silver crosses. That night men led by shoemaker Nicholas Melton set a guard on the treasury.

Next day an armed and unruly mob was about in the town and two Commissioners were seized and put in the stocks. Incited by priests of the deanery in town for an inquisition about the Ten Articles of the new Church of England, the mob assaulted the Bishop's Registrar and burned his books.

Word spread rapidly and on Tuesday some 3,000 men, including numbers from Caistor, mustered on the Wolds at Orford near Binbrook. One of the ringleaders was William Moreland, former monk of Louth Park Abbey.

St James' Church. Louth.

Engraving of St James's parish church, Louth, where the Lincolnshire Rising started on 1 October 1536.

scale than those on the higher Wolds. The more varied nature of the land, both for grazing and more labour intensive crops, resulted in a different system of farming. Cropping patterns were more diverse in these parishes.

Any description of early nineteenth-century agricultural development in the area draws heavily on the work of Arthur Young, Secretary of the Board of Agriculture, who made several tours describing farming activity. His *General View of the Agriculture of the County of Lincolnshire* was published in 1799, with a second edition in 1813. Thirty years before his *General View*, Young had been scathing in his opinion of farming practice on the Wolds: 'I saw little but what merited condemnation.' By 1799, he was more favourably disposed to the improvements that had taken place, with much of the 30 miles of warren from Spilsby to Caistor having been replaced by sheep and turnips.

'The farmers of this county are alive to improvements and ready to adopt any new instruments which promise utility', wrote Young, 'and they must be classed among the best cultivators in the kingdom'. Major improvements included 'the increase of turnips, and this has depended a good deal on the practice of paring and burning the wold sheep walks and gorse cover'. However, he did not see the less affluent side of Wold life, consequently his observations cannot always be taken as valid generalisations.

The 1801 Crop Returns provide useful details concerning the major arable crops grown. Across the northern Wolds turnips were the dominant crop

FIGURE 23. 30ft diameter waterwheel at Thoresway geared to a shaft under the road to drive machinery in farm barns.
DAVID ROBINSON

followed by barley, wheat and oats. In the cereal areas, wheat was less important than oats. Further south, barley was the most important crop, followed by turnips, oats and wheat. Only in the north were significant acreage of peas and beans grown.

The relative importance of the crops grown also indicates the prevalence of a mixed farming economy. On the northern and central Wolds, where 'turnips or rape' was the principal crop, the vast majority of this was turnip, an integral part of sheep farming. The introduction of turnips enabled sheep to be folded on the Wolds rather than being taken to the marshes to be fattened. The second largest acreage was barley, which although less profitable than wheat could, at that time, be grown more successfully on the thin chalky soils of the Wolds. Wheat yields were more variable; as a result, at the start of the nineteenth century, it was still considered to be a high risk crop by Wolds farmers.

Some cattle were kept. However, rabbits were of greater significance at the beginning of the nineteenth century. Rabbit warrens were often incorporated into the mixing farming system of the area. For instance, Mr Holdgate, the tenant of a 3,000 acre warren farm at Thoresway had 1,700 acres under silver rabbits, 850 acres of corn, 950 acres of grass, turnips and seed, and 700 sheep. He was also one of the first farmers in the area to experiment with a water-powered threshing mill. The majority of the warrens were well managed and profitable. However, changing fashion led to a decline in demand for silver grey rabbit fur, while rabbit meat as a cheap meat for the urban classes was replaced by mutton.

The higher prices obtained for grain, combined with significant improvements in cultivation techniques, led to large areas of marginal land being taken into cultivation. Philip Pusey in 1843 estimated that 230,000 acres on the Wolds had been 'added in our time to the cornlands of England'.

Alfred Tennyson recorded the same process of improvement in his poem *Northern Farmer (Old Style)*, referring to Thorganby Warren:

> *Dubbut looäk at the waäste: theer warn't not feäd for a cow,*
> *Nowt at all but bracken an' fuzz, an' looäk at it now,*
> *Warn't worth nowt a haäcre, an' now theer's lots o' feäd,*
> *Fourscore yows upon it an' some on it doon in seäd.*

On the land itself, improvements such as selective cross-breeding of animals were combined with higher levels of investment. At the same time, wheat yields rose from 20 to 24 bushels per acre in the 1790s to 28 to 32 bushels by the 1830s. National wheat yields did not reach this level until the 1860s.

The middle years of the nineteenth century saw improvements continue with the Wolds becoming an acclaimed centre of Victorian 'high farming'. The rise in arable production depended on a simultaneous improvement in the ways in which cattle were kept. During the mid and late nineteenth century, the provision of large scale and increasingly sophisticated methods of housing cattle was essential to ensure both quality livestock production and sustained soil

FIGURE 24. Lincoln
Longwool sheep on show.
DAVID ROBINSON

fertility. Improvements were made to farm buildings as well as to implements. At Worlaby, on the northern Wolds, Astley Corbett of Elsham Hall, erected in 1873 an impressive set of model farm buildings flanked by four pairs of cottages for the labourers. Christopher Turnor did likewise at Kirmond le Mire, while at Stourton Hall Farm, Great Sturton, the Liveseys developed a late Victorian mechanised farm with engine house and chimney, laid out so that slurry from the crewyards could be pumped into a chamber from which methane gas was collected.

The Wolds became well known for the quality of its sheep. As early as 1826, William Dawson of Withcall was producing heavy three-shear sheep. In 1847 Lincoln-Leicester crosses produced on the Wolds ranked 'amongst the most valuable breeds for the purposes assigned to them, and are shown in great perfection at the Lincoln, Caistor, Boston etc., great spring fairs'.

Sheep were clearly a major factor in maintaining high levels of profitability through the period. The 1864 catalogue for the Wyham and Cadeby estate was able to say (allowing for the estate agent's hyperbole): 'It is excellent wheat, turnip and barley land, and having so large a proportion of superior pasture land is peculiarly adapted for the production of lustre wool now so much in demand, and bearing such a high price in the manufacturing districts'. The Agricultural Crop and Livestock Returns provide a detailed picture from 1866. Across the whole Wolds in 1867, wheat occupied the largest acreage, followed by turnips, barley and oats. Sheep outnumbered cattle nearly fourteen fold. Turnips, grown as fodder for the sheep, remained the lynchpin of an economy based very much on sheep.

Analysis of three farms under the occupation of William Torr in 1869, at

Rothwell, Riby and Aylesby, provides a clear picture of the type of farming carried out by the more substantial Wold tenant farmers. He occupied 2,280 acres, farming under a four-course system with both cattle and sheep. The presence of a sizeable Shorthorn herd can be explained by his holding some 200 acres on the Humber Bank, an area which was equally well suited to cattle, unlike the chalk of the Wolds. His flock of sheep was famous throughout the country, indeed, 'The letting-books of the last twenty years show how much, and how widely, Aylesby blood is appreciated. A very large number of rams have gone to Ireland, and a few even to Jamaica and St Helena; while near at home Mr. Torr numbers amongst his customers residents in Scotland, Wales and most of the English counties', a picture of 'advanced ideas of good farming and successful breeding'.

In less than 75 years therefore, the Wolds had been transformed from an area

FIGURE 26. Threshing
team at Captain Hoff's
farm, Scremby.

FIGURE 27. Grange Farm tucked in the fold of the Wolds at Claxby by Willoughby.
DAVID ROBINSON

regarded by contemporaries as an agricultural backwater to one that epitomised the virtues of Victorian High Farming. The pages of the *Journal of the Royal Agricultural Society of England* were filled with fulsome commentaries on aspects of Wold farming, and its leading lights were regarded very highly by nineteenth-century agriculturalists.

However, from the second half of the 1870s, the profitability of agriculture declined. A series of poor harvests caused by bad weather reduced yields on farms. Previously poor harvests had, to some extent, been compensated for by high prices. But now prices remained static as a consequence of cheap imports. In 1870, Britain imported 28.8 million hundredweight of wheat, by 1875 the figure reached 42.6 million and by 1880 was more than 44 million. The combination of this flood of imports with a run of poor seasons put real pressure on farmers on the Wolds and had a traumatic effect on the farming communities.

While the occasional bad season might be expected and could be accommodated, it was the continuing series of poor harvests combined with low prices which brought many farmers to their knees. By 1879, the *Louth and North Lincolnshire Advertiser* reported: 'The agricultural interest of the county is feeling a very severe extent the bad years which have recently prevailed, and it is stated in official quarters that so many liquidations and compositions by farmers with their creditors as have been lately registered at the Lincoln County Court have not been known for a considerable number of years.'

There were exceptions, however. Even towards the end of the century Nathaniel Clayton, the Lincoln industrialist, treated his Withcall estate, purchased in the 1880s, as an experiment in highly capitalised and mechanised farming. Indeed, the area was still held in high regard by commentators: 'Large flocks of fine Lincoln, long wooled sheep are bred and fed on turnips and grass seed and numbers of large shorthorned cattle are bred and fed in the yards during the winter on roots, cake, corn and straw. By pursuing this system of farming the Wolds are kept in the highest state of cultivation that such a soil can be; they are made to produce magnificent crops of barley, excellent crops of turnips, and they turn out a class of sheep which have long been famous.'

It is no exaggeration to suggest that agriculture transformed the landscape of the Lincolnshire Wolds during the nineteenth century. A landscape characterised by rabbit warrens and sheep walks was converted into an extremely highly

FIGURE 28*(right)*. Pair of estate cottages at Kirmond le Mire, 1868.
PETER WILSON

FIGURE 29 *(below)*. Plan of Grange Farm, Kirmond le Mire, built for Christopher Turnor, 1868.

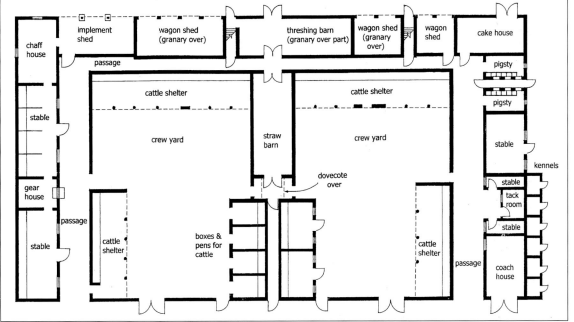

regarded area of mixed farming with an emphasis on wheat, barley, turnips and sheep. Until the early 1870s, progress seemed inexorable. The region was considered to be one of the foremost grain producing regions of the country. As an area of mixed farming with sheep integrated into rotations through the widespread use of turnips, it was considered sufficiently flexible to withstand all but the most serious of agricultural depressions. Its farmers were held up as examples of sound farming practice, and they certainly enjoyed long periods of sustained profitability. It was only in the final quarter of the century that this progress began to falter in the face of severe agricultural depression.

The first 40 years of the twentieth century were characterized by ongoing agricultural depression and population loss as out-migration exceeded natural increase. The lack of profitability in arable production was reflected in a steady shift in acreages from arable to grassland. From the high point of 1875, Lincolnshire as a whole had lost over 130,000 acres of arable land by 1938. Wolds farmers came increasingly to rely on livestock products.

The lack of profitability in Wolds farming was matched by a decline in the economic viability of the market towns. By the end of the 1930s, serious concerns were being expressed about the future of such towns as Market Rasen, Horncastle and Louth, all of which had populations lower than those recorded in the middle years of the nineteenth century. It was not until the revival in agricultural profitability following the Second World War that the decline of the previous 70 years was halted.

The Brocklesby Estate

The Earl of Yarborough's estate at Brocklesby is an excellent example of an aristocratic landscape developed from the late eighteenth century. It contains most of the elements of a time when conspicuous expenditure on landscape 'improvement' was very high indeed, and there was a strong emphasis on the central position of the country house in the life of the surrounding countryside. Brocklesby House was built in 1710 with further additions in 1807, 1827 and 1858, but suffered a major fire in 1898. In 1957–58, the then Lord Yarborough reduced the house and returned it to its original Georgian design while retaining the 1807 addition.

The present landscape was developed largely between 1770 and 1870, with some reworking of the formal gardens nearer to the Hall at the end of the nineteenth century. The park was laid out by Capability Brown in 1771–72. At the end of a two mile 'ride' from the House stands the magnificent Mausoleum. Its green-tinged copper dome today peeps out through the mature Cedar of Lebanon trees in the Mausoleum Woods just to the north of Great Limber village. The building, designed by James Wyatt as a memorial to Sophia Aufrere , the young wife of Charles Anderson Pelham (later the first baronet) was completed in 1792. From 1787 onwards,

Brockleby Mausoleum and Cedars of Lebanon.
DAVID ROBINSON

extensive areas of woodland were planted in a ten mile arc. The total cost of the work completed by Brown was £2,800, while the Mausoleum cost £20,000. In the 1790s Humphry Repton followed Brown to Brocklesby to carry out further work.

In 1849 Pelham's Pillar was built at a prominent point on the Wolds above Caistor, in line with the Mausoleum and Brocklesby House, to commemorate the planting of 12½ million trees on the estate between 1787 and 1823. Its impact today is reduced by the tall trees around it, yet it still provides an unparalleled vantage point for viewing the Brocklesby estate. These landscape 'improvements' emphasised the central position and importance of the House.

The second Earl was a director of the Manchester, Sheffield and Lincolnshire Railway. As a result, the railway line between Grimsby and Sheffield swept in a gentle arc to the north avoiding Brocklesby Park. The Earl arranged for Brocklesby Park Station to be built in the architectural style of his estate, linked to the House with an impressive approach through Newsham Lodge which had been built in 1815 to a design by Jeffry Wyatville. In 1864, the Memorial Arch spanning the road at the parish boundary between Brocklesby and Kirmington added further to the grandeur and glory of the Brocklesby estate, effectively producing a triumphal arch on one of the principal approaches to the House. It cost over £2,000, paid for by 'tenants and friends'. To either side are lodges in the Brocklesby style.

As well as work on the House and Park, the Yarboroughs also remodelled their two principal estate villages during the nineteenth century, Brocklesby and Great Limber, adorning their properties with the Pelham Buckle and painting them in 'Brocklesby blue'. Those properties nearest the House are the most ornate, while others further away, such as Swallow, which were remodelled during the same period, are plainer.

The Brocklesby Estate today is an excellent and relatively untouched example of the late eighteenth-and nineteen-century passion for 'place-making' – to use Brown's expression. The landscape is resonant with aristocratic values and attitudes from a previous age.

Charles Rawding

CHAPTER FIVE

Parliamentary Enclosure

Rex Russell

Enclosure is neatly described by J. H. Plumb in *England in the Eighteenth Century* as 'the replacement of two or three large open fields round a village, whose strips were owned individually but whose crops and stock were controlled by the community of owners, by smaller, individually owned fields where cropping and stock could be controlled by the owner'. The commonly stated reason for such a fundamental change in agricultural practice is recited in the preamble of an Act of Parliament required to effect the changes: 'And whereas the lands of the several Proprietors … lie intermixed and dispersed in small parcels, and are in general so inconveniently situated as to render Cultivation thereof difficult and expensive … and, in their present Situation, are incapable of much improvement …'

FIGURE 30. West Ashby before (1771) and after enclosure 1773.
REX RUSSELL

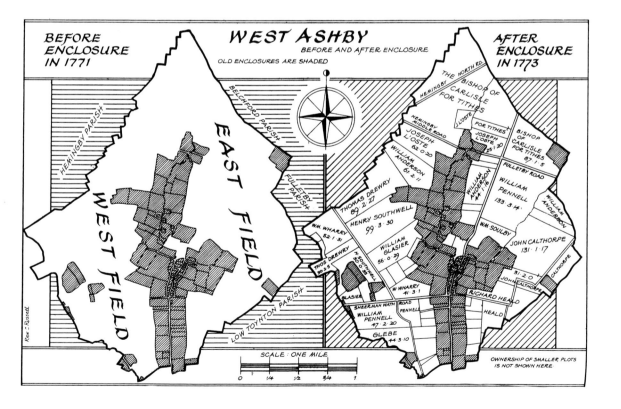

Enclosure of the open fields and commons of parishes on the Wolds by Acts of Parliament changed the look of the landscape. New straight roads with wide grass verges, up to 60 feet between the hedges in some cases, contrasted with the older, narrow and winding lanes with minimal verges. Good examples of enclosure roads across the former open fields, usually ignoring the contours of the land having been drawn by surveyors on a flat plan, are between West Ashby and Fulletby in the south of the Wolds and in Wootton parish in the north. New property boundaries drawn by the surveyors to identify private ownership were staked out, and owners also subdivided their allotments into fields. There was therefore a demand for 'quick' to plant the hundreds of miles of hawthorn hedges to create the now familiar rectangular pattern of fields and hedges, in contrast to irregular boundaries of the old closes near the village. The transformation was particularly marked in the northern and central areas of the Wolds, whereas the changes were less dramatic in the more intimate landscape of the south-eastern Wolds.

Ancient parish boundary hedges, where they still existed, were retained, along with those bordering the old village closes. A simple way of working out the age of a hedge on the Wolds is to count the number of species in a hundred yards section: one or two species indicates an age of about a hundred years, two to three species indicates an age of about two hundred years, and so on. Trees were also planted in new hedgerows, with careful spacing in fox hunting country where game coverts were also planted. All of the Wolds was hunted by the Brocklesby until the formation of the South Wold Hunt in 1822, with kennels at Harrington, Hundleby, Horncastle and Louth before establishing permanent kennels at Belchford in 1857.

There are some 90 parishes which lie entirely within the Wolds. In addition there are parishes on the western edge which extend into the Clay Vale, and on the east onto the Middle Marsh: about 25 of these have more than half their lands on the Wolds. Around thirty of the all-wold parishes were enclosed under Acts obtained from the 1760s to the early 1800s, most of them before 1800. The others were enclosed either by local agreement or where one person owned the whole parish, and therefore did not need to seek the assent of Parliament.

To obtain an Act it was necessary first for the major owners of land and rights of common to agree, it being 'much to their benefit'; second to have worked out what proportion of land should be allotted in lieu of tithes due to the vicar or rector and/or other tithe owners; and thirdly to have secured the services of commissioners and a surveyor who would carry out the work and determined their fees. All this, with other necessities including laying out roads, digging, fencing lands allotted in lieu of tithes, and solicitor's fees, could cost from £1 up to £6 per acre. Some examples, all enclosed in 1795, are Nettleton 3,332 acres costing £2,425, Ludford 2,167 acres – £2,256 and Tealby 2,609 acres – £3,339. The three commissioners for Tealby earned a total of £303, but the surveyor's fee was £587.

The Enclosure Award is the legal record of new land ownerships, as well as

FIGURE 31. Tealby before (1794) and after enclosure 1795.
REX RUSSELL

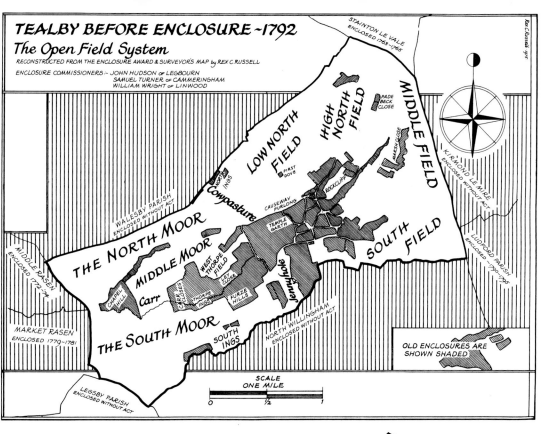

TEALBY BEFORE ENCLOSURE ~1792
The Open Field System

RECONSTRUCTED FROM THE ENCLOSURE AWARD & SURVEYOR'S MAP by REX C. RUSSELL

ENCLOSURE COMMISSIONERS:- JOHN HUDSON of LEGBOURN
SAMUEL TURNER of CAMMERINGHAM
WILLIAM WRIGHT of LINWOOD

Rex C. Russell 1975

STAINTON LE VALE
ENCLOSED 1763-1765

MIDDLE FIELD

PADE BECK CLOSE

HIGH NORTH FIELD

MARSH CLOSE

LOW NORTH FIELD

KIRMOND LE MIRE
ENCLOSED WITHOUT ACT

MAY INGS

FIRST DOVE

ROCKCLIFFE

Cowpasture

CAUSEWAY FURLONG

WALESBY PARISH
ENCLOSED WITHOUT ACT

TEMPLE GARTH

SOUTH FIELD

LUDFORD PARISH
ENCLOSED ~1790-1795

THE NORTH MOOR

MIDDLE MOOR

WEST THORPE FIELD

LEY CLOSE

MIDDLE RASEN
ENCLOSED 1772-74

Carr

CARR CLOSES

THORPE INGS

FURZE HILLS

Jenny hole

CHAPEL HILL

MARKET RASEN
ENCLOSED 1779-1781

THE SOUTH MOOR

SOUTH INGS

NORTH WILLINGHAM PARISH
ENCLOSED WITHOUT ACT

OLD ENCLOSURES ARE
SHOWN SHADED

LEGSBY PARISH
ENCLOSED WITHOUT ACT

SCALE
ONE MILE

0   ½   1

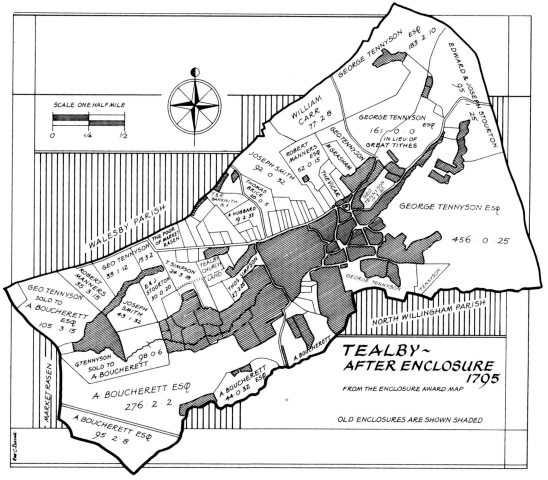

SCALE ONE HALF MILE

0   ¼   ½

GEORGE TENNYSON ESQ
183 · 2 · 10

EDWARD & JOSEPH STOURTON
95 · 1 · 25

WILLIAM CARR
77 · 2 · 8

GEORGE TENNYSON ESQ

GEORGE TENNYSON ESQ
161 · 0 · 0
IN LIEU OF GREAT TITHES

GEO TENNYSON

ROBERT MANNERS ESQ
52 · 0 · 15

JOSEPH SMITH
92 · 0 · 32

M. GRASHAM

THE VICAR

GEO TENNYSON

WALESBY PARISH

T. & R. BARKWITH
16 · 3

THOMAS BRICE
22 · 0 · 5

GEORGE TENNYSON ESQ
456 · 0 · 25

A. HUBBARD
19 · 2 · 33

GEO TENNYSON
33 · 1 · 12 · 1532

THE POOR OF MARKET RASEN

T. SIMPSON
24 · 3 · 18

TEALBY CHURCH LAND

GEORGE TENNYSON

ROBERT MANNERS
35 · 3 · 15

E. & J. STOURTON
30 · 0 · 20

THOS. SIMPSON
27 · 2 · 29

GEO TENNYSON
SOLD TO A. BOUCHERETT ESQ
105 · 3 · 15

JOSEPH SMITH
43 · 1 · 32

NORTH WILLINGHAM PARISH

G. TENNYSON
SOLD TO A. BOUCHERETT
98 · 0 · 6

MARKET RASEN

A. BOUCHERETT ESQ
276 · 2 · 2

A. BOUCHERETT
44 · 0 · 32 ESQ

A. BOUCHERETT

TEALBY ~ AFTER ENCLOSURE 1795

FROM THE ENCLOSURE AWARD MAP

OLD ENCLOSURES ARE SHOWN SHADED

A. BOUCHERETT ESQ
95 · 2 · 8

Rex C. Russell

FIGURE 32. Straight and wide-verged enclosure road in West Ashby parish.
DAVID ROBINSON

of roads and rights of way, where the number of people and acreage of land awarded reflects the ownerships and value of land and rights of common before enclosure – at Caistor there were 54 and at Tealby 49, in contrast to three in each of Swallow and Cabourne. However land could change hands during the enclosure process: at Searby on the north-west scarp of the Wolds (enclosed 1765) Edward Weston took the opportunity to purchase the properties of three other owners. Fewer landowners tended to result in large fields, whereas where there were many owners, fields were smaller, but removal of internal hedges in the last fifty years to create larger fields more efficient for modern agricultural machinery makes that difference now less obvious.

Ownership of one of the larger new allotments in the former open field enabled the building of new farmsteads away from the village for more efficient farming, typically given names such as Top Farm.

CHAPTER SIX

Transport in the Wolds

Neil Wright

For many centuries Lincolnshire was one of the remotest counties in England, and the Wolds were at the furthest side of the county. Transport improvements in the last 250 years have made them less remote than they used to be and in the twenty-first century their quiet beauty is being enjoyed by many visitors from outside the county. In the eighteenth century Turnpike Trusts were formed to improve the main roads of Lincolnshire. At the same time the creation of canals to Louth, Horncastle and Caistor, and improvements to the Rivers Witham and Ancholme, brought the benefits of waterway transport closer to the Wolds. In the middle of the nineteenth century, railways were built around the Wolds with branch lines to Horncastle and Spilsby, but only the Lincoln and Louth Railway line was built right through the heart of the Wolds.

Access from the Wolds to inland areas to the west and south was particularly difficult. The Fens and the wide valleys of the Rivers Witham and Ancholme formed a barrier of unenclosed land that was flooded for much of the year and had few roads across. South to Boston there was only one road, from Spilsby, and westwards the main ones were on the higher ridge between the Ancholme and Witham valleys from Wragby to Lincoln and Market Rasen to Gainsborough. A later road crossed the Ancholme at Glanford Brigg. In the winter months almost all of these routes were likely to be impassable in wet weather.

FIGURE 33. Stanmore Hill tollhouse on the corner of Halfpenny Lane, Louth.
DAVID ROBINSON

FIGURE 34. Turnpike milestone at Wold Newton.
DAVID ROBINSON

For centuries the people of each parish in England and Wales were responsible for the repair and maintenance of their local roads. Roads then did not have anything like today's tarmac surfaces but neither did they have the volume of traffic of the twenty-first century. Road repairs usually involved local people working a few days a year under the Parish Surveyor to fill deep ruts and to rake the surface level. In the Wolds, traffic on busy roads had worn down to the chalk and this provided a firmer surface than the soils beneath roads in the low-lying Marsh to the east, Fens to the south and Clay Vale to the west. These roads were often a muddy quagmire when wet and a dusty desert with hard baked ruts at other times. As far as possible, the use of roads for long distance traffic was kept to a minimum and coastal ports and creeks such as Barton on Humber, Barrow, Grimsby, Saltfleet, Wainfleet and Boston provided an easier link to the outside world. Some wharves, warehouses and other buildings of the old ports can still be seen at Boston, Wainfleet, Grimsby and Barton.

Road traffic in most of England started to increase in the seventeenth century

FIGURE 35. Louth to London Royal Mail coach stuck in the snow on Kenwick Top, winter 1835 by J. W. Pollard.

DAVID ROBINSON COLLECTION

and before long a new system was developed for maintaining long distance roads to replace the old system – the wear and tear were too much for the parishes. The solution was to make travellers pay for using main roads by the turnpike system. Local people would obtain an Act of Parliament to form a Turnpike Trust which allowed them to borrow and spend money on improving the road, and to charge the users a toll. The income was used to pay off the debt and to pay for maintenance. There was a different Trust for each road. Toll bars were put across the road near each end, at places along it and at junctions with other main roads. The bar consisted of a pole or pike that was raised or turned to one side, and it was from this that the name turnpike is believed to come. Next to each toll bar was a house for the toll collector, so that he could collect the tolls 24 hours a day. The Royal Mail and people going to Sunday services did not pay the tolls. Some turnpike trusts introduced better methods of making and repairing roads, but others simply used the old methods more often.

One of the first roads in Lincolnshire to be turnpiked was from Lincoln via Wragby to Baumber, on the way to Horncastle. The Trust was formed in 1739 by Wolds farmers who bought Scottish cattle for fattening on the Wolds before sending them for sale in London. In 1759 the Trust also took over the road from Wragby to Hainton on the way to Louth, and in 1780 extended their control to the edge of Louth itself.

Most of the main Turnpike Trusts for roads near the Wolds were formed by Acts obtained in 1765. Most were for roads on the surrounding lower-lying ground or to towns on the edge of the Wolds; few roads crossing over the Wolds were turnpiked. One Trust took on the road from Lincoln to Barton on Humber with branches to Caistor and Melton Ross. At Barton it met the ferry to Hull, and when the ferry was moved east to New Holland the turnpike was extended. Another Trust had the road from Boston to Alford via Spilsby. The biggest Trust in the area, the Dexthorpe, took over the road from Bawtry in Nottinghamshire (where it joined the Great North Road) via Gainsborough, Market Rasen and Louth to a junction with the Boston-Alford road. Only one road out of Grimsby was turnpiked in 1765, a short distance to Wold Newton; beyond there travellers used the unimproved road over the Wolds. People in Caistor had proposed turnpiking the road over the Wolds to Grimsby, but that was not done until a few years later. Roads from Louth to Saltfleet and Horncastle were turnpiked under an Act of 1770. In the late eighteenth century Louth was bigger and busier than Grimsby and had more need of good communications. The final link out of Louth to Grimsby was not turnpiked until 1803.

Travellers using turnpike roads would pay their toll and hope for a better road surface, as well as milestones to indicate distances between towns and sign-posts at junctions. Even though turnpike trusts were abolished over a century ago, when the new County Councils took responsibility for highways, some milestones and even a few toll houses remain, for example at Hallington near Louth. The standard of turnpiked roads did vary, but almost all were at least

FIGURE 36. A village carrier working to Louth on market days.

DAVID ROBINSON COLLECTION

FIGURE 37. The Lindsey
Rambler – a 1930
Chevrolet country bus.
DAVID ROBINSON COLLECTION

better than other roads. As the standard of main roads generally improved, the number of coaches using them steadily increased. This in turn led to the building of new and better inns for the use of travellers and where horses were changed. About 1784, regular stage-coach services began to run between London and Louth (via Boston) and Lincoln. The service to Lincoln was extended to Barton on Humber by 1791, where it met the ferry to Hull.

The Wolds gained some benefits from waterway improvements in the late eighteenth century. The Rivers Ancholme and Witham had been navigable for a long time but they both suffered from silting and a winding river course. After the winter rains there might be enough depth of water for boats to navigate them easily, but in a dry summer they could be too shallow for long periods. The problems on the Witham were largely sorted out in the 1760s and those of the Ancholme 40 years later. Both improvement schemes involved the digging of new straight channels and building sluices and locks where the rivers met the tidal waters of the Wash and the Humber respectively. These improvements also enabled drainage and enclosure of adjoining lands, including 40,000 acres of fenland between Boston and the southern edge of the Wolds, and better roads could be built across the reclaimed land to give access to and from the southern and western sides of the Wolds.

Three local canals also improved access to the Wolds. John Grundy did a survey for a navigation from Tetney Haven to Louth in 1756 but the Act was not obtained until 1763 and construction took place from 1765 to 1770. This access to the sea made Louth a busier port than Grimsby for many years. Some port buildings still remain at Louth Riverhead, as do most of the unusual barrel-shaped locks from Louth to Tetney.

FIGURE 38. A west-east drove road over the Wolds near Hallington.
DAVID ROBINSON

FIGURE 39. 14th century packhorse bridge at Utterby.
LINCOLNSHIRE WOLDS COUNTRYSIDE SERVICE

The other two canals to benefit the Wolds were less significant, and were part of the Canal Mania of the 1790s. A short stretch of canal had been built in 1787 from the River Witham to Tattershall and in 1792 an Act was obtained to extend it along the Bain Valley to Horncastle. This took a long time to build and was not opened until 1802, after a second Act to raise more money. At the other end of the Wolds, a canal from the Ancholme to Caistor was authorised in 1793 but it was only four miles long and terminated at Moortown. It did not even raise enough income to pay the interest on its debts. All of these canals lost trade when railways arrived about a half a century later.

For railway speculators in the Railway Mania of the late 1840s the main targets in Lincolnshire were the ports of Boston and Grimsby. The line from Lincoln via Market Rasen to Barnetby joined the main Manchester, Sheffield and Lincolnshire line to Grimsby through a low gap in the Wolds. East of the Wolds was the East Lincolnshire Railway from Boston via Alford and Louth to Grimsby and a line to the Humber ferry at New Holland. Nowhere on the Wolds was more that about ten miles from a railway station. All these lines opened in 1848, with a branch to Barton in 1849. Short branches to Horncastle and Spilsby were opened in 1855 and 1868 respectively. A proposal of 1886 to link those two branches with a line through the sandstone Wolds never came to fruition.

When the railways opened they had a devastating effect on long distance road traffic. Mail coach services stopped and passengers used the train instead. Only short distance road traffic survived, to take people to and from the nearest train station, and in Victorian times networks of village carriers' carts converged on Wold-edge towns on market days. The railways also took traffic from the canals and waterways, though it took longer to finally destroy that trade. Today pleasure boating and the heritage industry has grown to be the saviour of the surviving waterways.

In 1876 the Great Northern Railway opened the single track Lincoln to Louth Railway through the Wolds from Bardney to Louth using tunnels near Withcall and Benniworth, to shorten the route to the holiday coast at Mablethorpe with a branch line in 1877. Hubbard's Hills near Louth became a popular destination for Lincoln factory workers during Trip Week in July. However, railways serving the Wolds did not have a long life. Passenger services to Spilsby ceased in 1939

FIGURE 40. Louth to Bardney train at Benniworth Haven.

P. A. WELLS

and goods in 1958; passengers on the Louth-Bardney line in 1951 and goods in 1956; passengers on the Horncastle branch in 1954 and goods in 1971; and Louth lost its last railway link with the 'Beeching Axe' closure of the East Lincolnshire line from Firsby to Grimsby in 1970.

During the twentieth century, cars and lorries took over nearly all transport in the Wolds, and Lindsey County Council, as the highway authority, had responsibility for making and repairing the road network. The former RAF bomber base at Kirmington became Humberside Airport and now handles an increasing volume of tourist traffic. On the other hand village bus services, the successor to the carrier's cart, have diminished or disappeared, and for most people and businesses in the Wolds the motor vehicle is the only means of transport. The A180 slices through the northern chalk hills, with a dual carriageway link from Melton Ross to the Humber Bridge, and Caistor and Louth have road bypasses, the latter through the eastern edge of the AONB.

CHAPTER SEVEN

Holes in the Wolds

David Robinson

It is perhaps surprising how many holes have been dug in the Wolds, well over a hundred and fifty large and small: clay for bricks and cement, sandstone for building, ironstone for building and smelting, chalk for building, hardcore, agricultural lime and cement, and sands and gravels for aggregate. Many of the holes have disappeared from view, having succumbed to landfill, or landscaping for recreation, but others are now nature reserves or have been designated as Sites of Special Scientific Interest or Regionally Important Geological Sites, but three of the largest, at Melton Ross, Nettleton and South Ferriby are still working extracting chalk.

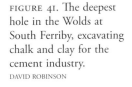

FIGURE 41. The deepest hole in the Wolds at South Ferriby, excavating chalk and clay for the cement industry.
DAVID ROBINSON

The earliest exploitation of stone for building was by the Romans, using Spilsby Sandstone for the fort walls at Horncastle taken from a quarry four miles away at Holbeck. Later the walls were robbed to rebuild St Mary's church

FIGURE 42. Workers in the Mill Hill chalk quarry, Claxby by Willoughby in the 1920s, and remains of a lime-burning kiln.
BOTH DAVID ROBINSON COLLECTION

and the Manor House. The distribution of stone-built churches using Spilsby Sandstone (usually referred to as a greenstone), Claxby Ironstone and Chalk reflects the surface outcrops of those rocks, mainly on hillsides. The fifty or so churches built of the green and well-cemented sandstone are to be found in the southern Wolds round the Lymn valley and on the western side of the Wolds as far north as North Willingham. These churches are generally small, serving small parishes on rather poor, sour soils.

The source of stone for St Margaret's at Somersby seems to have been a small roadside quarry half a mile to the west, where occasional stone was still being cut in the late 1960s (see illustration on p. 12). St Helen's, West Keal, partly rebuilt in 1881–84, probably took the stone from a roadside outcrop only a few hundred yards away. A feature of cut blocks of the Spilsby Sandstone, particularly the green beds, is that the outer surface develops a hard patina, but if this is broken, as it can be on warm south-facing walls by mason bees, erosion by weathering can be quite rapid. And where there is little cementing content in the stone and more iron, it can be quarried virtually as a sand, as was done in a small pit across the river from the watermill at Donington on Bain.

The walls of Bolingbroke Castle were built almost entirely of Spilsby Sandstone, including some of the iron rich yet well cemented layers, probably from the side of Kirkby Hill to the west. Much of the castle was pulled down after the Civil War, and what is seen today is largely the result of archaeological excavations in the 1960s. Spilsby Sandstone was also used for the basic walling of churches in the Lincolnshire Marsh, where no stone was available, using imported limestone which could be carved for window tracery and other decorative features. Usually this was oolitic Lincolnshire Limestone from the west of the county. The stone for the spire of St James's, Louth, built in 1501–1515, came from quarries on Wilsford Heath near Ancaster, but that for Louth Park Abbey was Magnesian Limestone from south Yorkshire.

Churches of ironstone – there are 20 or more where it is the main building material – are grouped in the north-central Wolds within easy reach of the

FIGURE 43. South wall of Bolingbroke Castle built of Spilsby Sandstone cut from the nearby hillside.
LINCOLNSHIRE WOLDS
COUNTRYSIDE SERVICE

outcrops of Claxby Ironstone, but also extending north to Brocklesby and east as far as Yarburgh in the Middle Marsh. Ironstone was also used for a new church in the nineteenth century, that of St Mary and St Gabriel at Binbrook, designed by James Fowler of Louth in 1869 (see illustration on p. 98). The opencast quarrying and underground mining of ironstone at Claxby and Nettleton for the Scunthorpe steelworks is described elsewhere (p. 67).

Small chalk masonry was often used for the core of church walls, and survives in the ruined St Andrew's at Calceby and the remains of the chancel walls at Louth Park Abbey. However, it was really only the 1m (3ft) bed of the hard grey Totternhoe Stone which could be used for ashlar work, as seen in churches from Legbourne in the south to Utterby and Hawerby in the north. It was only that part of the eastern edge of the Wolds where the Totternhoe stone was available. It was also used for farm barns at North Ormsby and Wold Newton, with an isolated example of a fourteenth century manor house at Keelby. Near North Ormsby is the only example of flint walling in the Wolds, the lower walls of an isolated barn on the minor road west of the abbey site.

There were more than 40 chalk quarries or lime pits around the fringes of the Wolds, half of them along the old cliff line on the east and half on the west where the chalk could be exploited on the crest of the escarpment. They had a dual purpose: to supply hardcore for roads, particularly on the Lincolnshire Marsh, and burnt lime for agriculture. Those on the east extended from Candlesby to Thornton Curtis, three of them now nature reserves (Candlesby Hill, Mill Hill, Claxby by Willoughby – where there is a restored limekiln, and Fir Hill, Little Cawthorpe). The largest limepits were at Louth: Saturday Pits near the southern boundary of the parish, so named because the market was moved there in the plague years of the seventeenth century; the quarry which started as the source of stone for Louth Park Abbey and is now the site of the cattle market; and the limeworks off Grimsby Road on the north side of the town. Just south of Louth the large chalk hole at Kenwick Top has just reached the end of its life as a landfill site.

On the western escarpment the chalk pits are in two groups, the first from Dalby Hill, Brinkhill, Tetford and Belchford (a shallow pit on the crest alongside the Bluestone Heath Road) and Red Hill, Goulceby, now a Local Nature Reserve. The land at Red Hill had been allotted under the Asterby and Goulceby Enclosure Award in 1778 to the Overseers of Highways for digging chalk for road-making and repairs. The second group is along the northern scarp from Nettleton (the quarry on the side of the Nettleton Beck having been used to supply lime as a flux in steelmaking) and sizeable pits at Grasby, Bigby and Elsham to South Ferriby, with four along the Barton Cliff facing the Humber. Those five in the north were, and one still is, associated with the cement industry. The one still working on Middlegate Lane, South Ferriby is a spectacular hole cut down through the Chalk and the thin Carstone and Red Chalk (all that remains there of the Lower Cretaceous rocks) into the grey Kimmeridge Clay and so able to supply both chalk and clay for the cement works at Ferriby Sluice. The hole is some 90m (300ft) deep with the bottom probably lower than the River Humber.

By far the largest, and still expanding, hole in the Wolds is the chalk quarry at Melton Ross, covering about two-thirds of a square mile. It lies between the A18 and the A180, and alongside the railway through the Barnetby gap. Its main output is lime. In sharp contrast is the multitude of dimples in the chalk tops, most now ploughed out or scrubbed over with vegetation. Many are away from tracks, in the middle of a field or at the junction of two or three fields. Chalk was dug out in the autumn, spread on the fields to weather over the winter and then ploughed in to replenish the lime which had been leached downwards by rain. Perhaps the easiest way to see exposures of chalk is in the vertical-sided cutting made for the A15 approaching the Humber Bridge, where the bedding and layers of flint nodules of the Welton Chalk are clearly visible.

Of other Wolds rocks, some Tealby Limestone can be found in walls of churches, cottages and property boundaries around Tealby and Donington on Bain, but the most common building material in the nineteenth century was brick. Where Kimmeridge Clay was accessible in the Bain valley there were brick and tile works at Horncastle (2), Goulceby and Donington on Bain, and at the western edge of the parish of Fulletby alongside the River Waring. On the eastern side of the Wolds, and using glacial clays, were eight brickyards in Louth and one at South Elkington, the latter where a chalk paste was mixed

FIGURE 44. 19th century farm barn at North Ormsby built with cut blocks of chalk.
DAVID ROBINSON

FIGURE 45. Chalk quarry on Mansgate Hill, Nettleton.
LINCOLNSHIRE WOLDS COUNTRYSIDE SERVICE

with the clay to produce a whitish brick for building South Elkington Hall in 1841. Within the Wolds were short-lived brickyards using silts laid down in proglacial lakes at Tetford and Petterhills (between Wold Newton and East Ravendale). The localised Hundleby Clay in the southern Wolds was used at Hundleby and East Keal. Except where surviving as fishing lakes, most pits where clay was dug have been filled in and some built over.

Brick had been in demand for new farm buildings, houses and cottages in the growth years of the nineteenth century, but small enterprises closed when demand declined and cheap Fletton bricks became available by rail. Only one brickworks in Horncastle and one in Louth survived into the twentieth century, both being fatally damaged by flooding from the Bain and the Lud in May 1920. (There is a display about local brickmaking in Louth Museum.)

Exploitation of sand and gravel for aggregate left extensive rather than deep holes, often flooded as in the Bain valley and turned to recreational use. Within the Wolds, had it not been for the digging of gravel at Welton le Wold from the 1930s to the 1970s the clues to understanding the ice ages in eastern England might never have been found. A disused pit in glacial sands alongside the A16 near South Thoresby was reactivated in 1969 to line the gas pipeline trench across the Wolds; an attempt to save it as a nature reserve with orchids and sand martins failed, and it became yet another landfill site.

Nettleton Mines

The journey today from Nettleton south towards Normanby le Wold takes you over the roof of the county. A pause by Nettleton Top Farm will give dramatic views over a peaceful countryside where for long periods the only sounds are the wind through the trees and birdsong. However, 50 years ago it was a different story. Here, beneath your feet, about 28 metres down, are the tunnels of the former ironstone mines and for 40 years in the middle of the twentieth century these hillsides were the scene of great industrial activity.

The presence of ironstone here had long been known. Many parish churches in nearby villages, together with houses, are built of it. Furthermore, this was not the first ironstone mine in the area. At Claxby, a mile to the south, an underground mine opened in 1868 and worked for 17 years.

There were two mines at Nettleton. Digging started on the first, the Top Mine, in 1928, but production did not start until 1934. By 1957 the mine was almost exhausted and work began on opening up Bottom Mine, 1.5 kilometres to the east. Top Mine closed in 1959 as Bottom Mine came into production. Bottom Mine closed in 1968.

Underground gallery in the Nettleton Iron Mine, 1960s.
DAVID ROBINSON

The mine buildings can still be seen at Nettleton Top. The mine adits ran straight out of the hillside and the workshops, offices, staffrooms and stables were set on the scarp slope of the Wolds, just below its crest. From there an aerial ropeway ran to Holton le Moor railway station, 2.4 kilometres to the west, from where the ore was loaded into wagons for its journey to the steelworks at Scunthorpe. When Bottom Mine opened a road replaced this ropeway and transport was by large dump trucks.

Underground, the principal motive power was diesel locomotives running on a narrow gauge tramway. However, in Top Mine horses were used for short hauls from working faces to the main headings. In 1954 there were twelve horses and, in 1959, eight. Nettleton Bottom Mine used locomotives exclusively and so the horses were retired with the closure of Top Mine.

The opening of Nettleton Bottom Mine required the building of a new mine railway to link the mine with the earlier buildings. New tunnels ran through Top Mine, emerging briefly into the open air to cross the head of a small valley before running underground again to reach the valley of the Nettleton Beck. Again emerging into the open air, the railway crossed the valley on a high embankment before reaching the adit leading to the mine workings.

Mining was by the method known as pillar and stall. This entailed leaving pillars of rock between excavated areas to support the roof and the ground above. However, because of continued high demand from the steelworks and because of delays in starting production from Bottom Mine, production had to be maintained. This was achieved in two ways. Firstly, in Top Mine many of the pillars were robbed, that is they were removed. The effect of this can clearly be seen in the fields over the top. The ground is very uneven indicating the collapses underground caused by the pillars being removed. The second method was to quarry ironstone from the valley sides at the places where it outcropped. The valley sides today look natural but have, in fact, been partly created by the hand of man.

Mining came to an end in 1968 with reserves in Bottom Mine hardly touched. The reason was the import of foreign ores with a far higher iron content. Almost two hundred men were made redundant and the valleys returned to the peaceful state in which we see them today. There are remnants to be seen – roadways, buildings and bricked-up adits as well as the embankment across the Nettleton Bottom valley.

Stewart Squires

CHAPTER EIGHT

The Wolds at War

Terry Hancock

Nowhere in Lincolnshire in 1938 were preparations for war more visible than the group of tall masts being erected on top of the Wolds at Stenigot. The Air Ministry described them as a Radio Direction Finding stations, something the public (and the Germans) seemed to accept. There were already radio masts at the Royal Navy's wireless station at Cleethorpes and the GPO's North Sea Radio station at Trusthorpe. However, the Stenigot structures were one of the first radar stations in the country and, indeed, the world. The station's official title was Air Ministry Experimental Station Type 1, which again gave no indication of its real purpose. By August 1939 the work was finished and the four 360 feet high steel transmitter towers and four 280 feet high wooden receiver towers dominated the Wolds. They were one of 20 original Chain Home long-distance radar stations in a chain from the Isle of Wight eastwards and northwards around the coast to guard against German bombers. Their value to the defence of Britain in the

FIGURE 46. The remaining Stenigot mast, one of eight of the world's first radar chain. It was retained to train RAF aerial erecters.
TERRY HANCOCK

coming months cannot be overestimated. They sent out radio beams in a 120 degrees arc to a distance of some 100 miles to detect approaching enemy aircraft. The 140 operational personnel were housed in a small hutted camp to the east, at New Buildings near Withcall, some of the buildings are still there.

A shortcoming of the CH stations was that they could only search out to sea and above about 10,000 feet. Once aircraft crossed the coast or approached below that height, they could not be seen on the radar screens. This required keeping track of aircraft by the visual sightings of the Observer Corps, which had been formed in 1925. The Lincoln group was established in 1936, with 33 reporting posts in Lincolnshire and neighbouring counties. Since the posts needed good all-round visibility, it is not surprising that several were situated on the Wolds – at Swallow, Burgh on Bain, Baumber, Binbrook, Louth, Alford, Tetford and Winceby. Observers with binoculars and a 'post instrument' would report the course, height, map reference and type of aircraft seen (or heard, at night or in bad visibility) to the Lincoln centre where all reports were co-ordinated, to give the aircraft's track across the county, and passed to the RAF. The observer posts usually comprised a small wooden hut and an open-topped brick and wood structure. Even when later radar with a 360 degrees search pattern entered service it could not pick up very low-flying aircraft, so the Observer Corps, granted the Royal prefix in 1941, performed a valuable service beyond the end of the Second World War, particularly in helping friendly aircraft unsure of their position.

An early version of the Observer Corps, manned by Special Constables, had existed from 1916 to the end of the First World War, specifically to report the arrival over Britain of German airships, the Zeppelins. As Lincolnshire was a favourite entry point, several airfields in the west of the county were established to operate Home Defence fighter aircraft. The distance from the coast was to allow

FIGURE 47. A 101 Squadron Lancaster bomber prepares for take-off at RAF Ludford Magna sometime in 1944. Ground crews worked in the open, often in muddy conditions in the winter.
101 SQUADRON

the fighters to attain operational altitude by the time the airship had travelled inland. To accommodate aircraft patrolling the coast, if a raid was expected, Landing Grounds were created. These were usually just two fields with the hedge between to give an L-shaped landing and take-off area. They were manned by only a couple of airmen who would light a flare path if necessary. Landing Grounds on the Wolds were at Cuxwold, Kelstern and Moorby. Elsham aerodrome was actually a flight station for 33 Home Defence Squadron, with hangars and living quarters. The Squadron's FE2b fighters were airborne when there was a Zeppelin raid and flew patrols between raids, without the benefit of radio or radar. Elsham aerodrome and the Landing Grounds quickly disappeared after 1918.

The Wolds were not at first considered an ideal location for airfields because of the risk of low cloud. However, in 1938–1939 work started on a new airfield near Binbrook, with permanent brick buildings to a design approved by the Council for the Protection of Rural England and the Fine Arts Commission. This was the only one of its type on the Wolds, subsequent stations being of the wartime hutted variety. Planned as a bomber airfield, Binbrook opened in June 1940, just in time to receive two Fairey-Battle-equipped squadrons returning from the Battle of France, where they had taken many casualties. They were soon attacking French ports housing invasion barges, re-equipping with the more-effective Wellington medium-bomber later that year to attack targets in Germany. Wellingtons from Binbrook operated over mainland Europe until the advent of the RAF's heavy bombers required the construction of hard-surfaced runways, and the station closed from September 1942 to May 1943 for the work to be carried out. The new runways were soon put to use as the Lancaster bombers of 460 (Royal Australian Air Force) Squadron moved in, Binbrook remaining the Squadron's home for the rest of the war. There is a roadside memorial to the Squadron on the edge of Binbrook Village.

FIGURE 48. Royal Observer Corps post near Alford: a simple hut with air-raid shelter and privy.

C. S. PARKER

FIGURE 49. The 250ft radar mast at Skendleby Top. On a good day aircraft could be plotted over Paris. The station closed in 1957.
D. CATON

Elsham Wolds, on the site of the old Landing Ground, joined the bomber war against Germany in July 1941 with hutted accommodation and workshops and temporary, metal-clad hangars. 103 Squadron was its unit, flying Wellingtons, Halifaxes (briefly) and Lancasters until the end of the war, a second Lancaster squadron joining from 1943 to 1944. Other bomber airfields on the Wolds were Kirmington with 166 Squadron, opened in early 1942, Ludford Magna with 101 Squadron in June 1943, and Kelstern with 625 Squadron in October 1943.

In addition to bombing, 101 Squadron had the task of searching out the German night-fighters' radio frequencies and jamming them; that was done by an eighth, German-speaking crew member. The Lincolnshire bomber squadrons suffered heavy losses, 317 men failing to return from the Nuremburg raid, Bomber Command's costliest, on the night of 30 March 1944. Apart from the comforts of Binbrook, the airmen had little in the way of creature comforts in the Nissen huts in which they lived and worked during the bleak Wolds winters. Kelstern closed just before the war ended, and apart from Binbrook, the other airfields had closed by 1947. Little now remains at Ludford, Elsham and Kelstern except patches of runway and perimeter track and a few buildings, but there are Squadron memorials at all three, and at Binbrook and Kirmington.

In the first four years of the war the bombs for the Lancasters came from dumps in the west of the county, but in January 1943 Market Stainton Hall and its grounds, plus fields in the locality, were taken over for bomb storage by 233 Maintenance Unit. The bombs were delivered by road and by rail, via Withcall and Hallington stations. Ammunition was also stored along the grass verges of roads and lanes around the village, often unguarded. Old RAF huts can still be seen in the Hall grounds and neighbouring fields.

Radar developed rapidly during the war and a new type, the Chain Home Low, came into service in 1941, with revolving scanners which could search through 360 degrees, and could pick up aircraft at lower heights. These complimented longer range masts at Stenigot. A Chain Home Low station

FIGURE 50. No 11 Squadron Lightning fighters at RAF Binbrook, 1957.

C. S. PARKER

opened at Skendleby on the southern edge of the Wolds, together with Stenigot and a Ground Controlled Interception radar at Orby, enabled night-fighters from Coleby Grange to intercept the, by then, rare attacks crossing the Lincolnshire coast. Radar was also of great help to friendly aircraft.

After the war Stenigot and Skendleby remained as part of the country's air defence network, but the Cold War encouraged rapid radar development, and despite Skendleby's operations room being buried underground in the early 1950s, both were closed by 1958. However, Skendleby found a new role as the Regional Seat of Government for the East Midlands with an underground bunker system to house a cabinet minister and high-ranking civil servants and military officers, in the event of a nuclear war; thankfully this never happened and Skendleby was sold off following the end of the Cold War but its massive air intakes and filters on an earth mound still dominate the site. The radar scanner now operating at Claxby Top is a Civil Aviation Authority facility, tracking airliners and other aircraft over eastern England and the North Sea.

Of the Wolds airfields, only Binbrook survived the post-war rundown, because of its permanent buildings and proximity to the east coast with a shorter distance to possible Russian targets. Lancasters were replaced by the slightly improved Lincoln until 1951, when Binbrook became the first RAF station to receive the revolutionary new jet bomber, the Canberra, which operated until 1959. The airfield then went into a period of 'care and maintenance', before becoming a fighter station in 1962. It was first equipped with Javelin fighters, soon replaced by the last all-British fighter, the superb English Electric Lightning, at the time one of the best interceptors in the world. Two squadrons flew from Binbrook, defending the V-bomber bases and the Thor Intercontinental Ballistic Missile bases established by the RAF from 1958 to 1963 on disued airfields in eastern England. One of those sites was on Ludford Magna airfield, and its three Thors would have been upright and nuclear-armed for the Cuban missile crisis in 1962. The Lightnings operated until 1988, by which time the rest of the RAF's Lightnings

FIGURE 51. 625 Squadron memorial when newly erected on Kelstern bomber base, with ruin of the control tower in right background.
DAVID ROBINSON

had been replaced, and Leeming in Yorkshire took over Binbrook's role. Binbrook's weather record, and the need for a fighter airfield further north, led to its closure, and those well-built airfield buildings are now gently deteriorating, though the married quarter site became Brookenby village.

It was the Royal Observer Corps which provided the last air defence presence on the Wolds, with posts at Alford, Baumber, Burgh on Bain and Louth. The Corps had abandoned its aircraft reporting role in the early 1960s, and had taken on a new role of plotting nuclear explosions and the subsequent spread of radioactive fallout. This role was performed from small underground bunkers until the end of the Cold War made them redundant, and the Corps stood down in 1991. The underground posts are still mostly in existence, and south of Burgh on Bain, on the corner of the Caistor High Street and the road to South Willingham, one can still see an aircraft reporting post on top of the mound of the bunker.

Storms over the Wolds

There is a belief that storms tend to lodge in the Bain valley against the western edge of the Wolds and that the higher ground helps to set off thunderstorms in unstable atmospheric conditions. Heavy rainfall on the watershed could affect the Bain and its tributaries flowing south and/or the streams which focus eastwards on Louth. The unusually heavy rainfall of 31 December 1900 only affected the Bain and caused significant flooding in Horncastle. The so-called 'cloudburst' of Saturday 29 May 1920 affected both systems and 6.3 inches of rain was recorded at Horncastle. The Bain burst its right bank above Horncastle, the water was funnelled between high buildings at the corner of Prospect Street and West Street, demolished three cottages in West Street to return to its normal course, but there was no loss of life. That was not the case in Louth, however, where the disastrous flash flood claimed 23 lives.

Up to five inches of rain fell within the 22 square mile catchment area of the River Lud west of Louth, depositing some 12 million tons of water in less than three hours that Saturday afternoon. Even greater falls

Gulley in the chalk escarpment at Red Hill first formed on 29 May 1920 and re-excavated by storm rain on 25 June 2007.
DAVID ROBINSON

were recorded at Stenigot (6.3 inches), at Warren Farm, Welton le Wold (6 inches) and in Welton village (4.7 inches in 2½ hours), yet Louth itself had only 1.42 inches. Such was the intensity of the downpour that gullies up to six feet deep were scoured into the chalk at Warren Farm. Running water ploughed trenches in the stony Wolds roads, and the bridge on the Louth-Horncastle road at Maltby was completely swept away.

Red Hill, Goulceby on the edge of the Wolds escarpment was near the epicentre of the most intense rainfall. It filled the old chalk quarry, breaking through the roadside edge as a washout and carved a gully in the field on the south side of the road, creating a waste-fan towards Goulceby. Despite years of ploughing the line of the gully can still be identified by soil colouration and crop marking.

The Wolds catchment of the Lud has eight tributary valleys, the run-off from which converges immediately west of Louth. In Hubbard's Hills the river suddenly became a 15-feet deep torrent, sweeping dead animals and debris before it. At the footbridge by Little Welton trees and other flotsam choked the channel and muddy water filled the valley upstream to a depth of 30 feet. At five o'clock the logjam broke and a wall of water 14 feet high joined the rushing water from Hubbard's Hills and swept towards an unsuspecting town where families were preparing afternoon tea. Within minutes the Lud rose seven feet and then fifteen feet, demolishing nearly all before it, flooding streets and properties over six feet deep, up to the ceiling in some cottages. Fifty houses were damaged beyond repair, 200 needed rebuilding and a further 500 were affected by flood water; 23 people ranging from 1 to 82 years of age were drowned, and 800 were made homeless. It was a national disaster.

Just over forty years later, on 7 October 1960, another thunderstorm, a cumulonimbus cloud towering to 40,000 feet, lodged against the south-west edge of the Wolds near Horncastle, with the town itself receiving 7.24 inches of rain in six hours. This time it was the left bank tributaries of the Bain, the River Waring and its diminutive tributary the Scrafield Beck which brought flooding to the town. The silt-filled canalised section of the Waring in the town was overflowing by mid-day and water depths in the town soon reached six feet and even eight feet in places, and two footbridges were carried away. Most of the streets were clear of water by eight o'clock in the evening. South of the town the small Scrivelsby and Haltham Becks carried the equivalent of the normal discharge of the River Thames at Teddington for a short time before subsiding.

All that in contrast to the mean annual rainfall on the high Wolds of 27 to 28 inches.

David Robinson

CHAPTER NINE

The Wolds in Literature and Art

Terry Miller

We call the southern Wolds 'Tennyson Country', yet it is noticeable how gently Lincolnshire holds Tennyson to itself. His home is not 'themed' – you cannot visit his birthplace, but a son of the Lincolnshire Wolds he was, nurtured in the Arcadian landscape of Somersby. His genius was deeply influenced by those rural landscapes and he expressed for his age, and for ours too, those quintessential qualities of rural England.

Yet it is no coincidence that, at the same time as the land was becoming 'landscape plotted and pieced' in the hands of the surveyors, with hedgerow geometry, there blossomed a new awareness that we call 'Romantic'. The love of the '*landschap*' – after the Dutch – was taken to heart by the English and whether captured by Constable or DeWint, or described by Wordsworth or Tennyson, is powerfully symbolic of what we hold dear – the inhabited tamed landscape, where people and nature co-exist. The more nature has been 'commodified', the more we fiercely defend this lost Eden. We see this well expressed in Peter DeWint's 'Lincolnshire Cornfield near Horncastle' c1815 – unbounded land under an unbounded sky, as nature intended it.

Our interest in nature, of course, preceded that flowering of awareness, but our pride was more utilitarian. There were few things more inspiring than a productive land, yielding good harvests, for on this was the wealth, and not a little greed, of the nation founded. Daniel Defoe, that great traveller, journeying round the country early in the eighteenth century as a secret agent, reflected on the landscape between Caistor, Spilsby and Horncastle noting that *...all this country is employ'd in husbandry, in breeding and feeding innumerable droves and flocks of cattle and sheep*.

It was that wealth from the land which drove the agricultural improvers to transform dramatically the open heaths to the enclosed fields regarded as characteristically English today, and now lament their passing from the 1950s as fields gave way to arable prairies. The improver saw the open pastoralist grazing as a bleak and heath-like landscape – *warren for thirty miles from Spilsby to beyond Caistor*, said Arthur Young of the Wolds in 1799.

Driven by the agricultural revolution, the transformation of the open landscape progressed with great speed. For a thousand years since the arrival of Saxon and Dane the integrated farming system of water meadows, open strip-field rotations, rough grazing, sheep walks and heathland had shaped the land. Then Acts of Parliament gave ownership to the former 'open fields, commons, and waters', commuting and sweeping away tithes, providing better roads and drains. Tennyson's 'Northern Farmer (Old Style)' took pleasure in those changes that multiplied his resources:

> *Dubbut looäk at the waäste: theer warn't not feäd for a cow:*
> *Nowt at all but bracken an' fuzz, an' looäk at it now –*
> *Warnt worth nowt a haäcre, an' now theer's lots o' feäd,*
> *Fourscore yows upon it an' some on it doon in seäd.*

In April 1830 William Cobbett in the *Rural Rides* on his journey from Boston to Horncastle described the sight of a man ploughing near Scamblesby:

> The vale in which it lies is very fine land. A hazel mould, rich and light too. I saw a man ploughing for barley, after turnips, with one horse: the horse did not seem to work hard, and the man was singing: I need not say that he was young…

He described the Wolds land with some praise:

> This is very fine corn country: chalk at bottom: stony near the surface in some places: here and there a chalk pit in the hills: the shape of the ground somewhat like that of the broadest valleys in Wiltshire; but the fields not without fences as they are there: fields from 15 to 40 acres: the hills not downs, as in Wiltshire, but cultivated all over. The houses white and thatched, as they are in all chalk countries. The valley at Scamblesby has a little rivulet running down it, just as in all the chalk countries. The land continues nearly the same to Louth, which lies in a deep dell, with pastures

FIGURE 52. A March scene along the Bluestone Heath Road above Tetford by Eric Littlewood.
DAVID ROBINSON COLLECTION

on the surrounding hills, like those I once admired at Shaftesbury, in Dorsetshire… We left Louth on the morning of Thursday 15th, and got to Barton-on-Humber by about noon, over a very fine country, large fields, fine pastures, flocks of those great sheep, of from 200 to 1000 in a flock; and here in Barton we arrived at the northern point of this noble county, having never seen one single acre of waste land, and not one acre that would be called bad land in the south of England.

Yet Cobbett had earlier decried the poverty that might have resulted from the enclosure and improvement of the land, concentrating wealth in fewer hands, and reducing the smallholder to landless labourer, when he wrote of his journey near Holbeach in the Fens:

…and seeing the fatness of the land, and the fine grass, and the never-ending sheep lying about like fat hogs stretched in the sun, and seeing the abject state of the labouring people, I could not help exclaiming, "God has given us the best country in the world; our brave and wise and virtuous fathers, who built all these magnificent churches, gave us the best government in the world, and we, their cowardly and foolish and profligate sons, have made this once-paradise what we now behold!"

This is reminiscent of John Clare, perhaps our greatest naturalist-poet, who bitterly felt the changes to his beloved landscape down to the very ivy on a post: 'Took a walk in the fields saw an old wood stile taken away from a favourite spot which it had occupied all my life. The posts were overgrown with ivy and it seemed so akin to nature and the spot where it stood as tho it had taken it on lease for an undisturbed existence. It hurt me to see it was gone for my affections claim a friendship with such things…'

FIGURE 53. Harrington Hall from the 'high hall garden' of Tennyson's poem 'Maud'.
DAVID ROBINSON

Precious fragments of small pre-enclosure field systems with sinuous species-rich hedges still survive in the Wolds, alongside the new landscape, mainly in places where mechanical juggernauts have no advantage and animal husbandry is more appropriate.

Romantic sensibilities are ambivalent about this transformation. The new mood on the one hand sought out wilder places, less dominated by human hands, and on the other the intimate, the local, perhaps more akin to a classical Arcadian vision of Giorgione and Claude Lorraine. One artist, claimed by Lincolnshire as one of their own, who embraces the classical quattrocento Renaissance formalism, the utilitarian admiration of good land, and the new emergent feelings about landscape was George Stubbs (1724–1806). The son of a Liverpool currier, he came to Horkstow in 1758 and took a farmhouse with his niece Mary Spencer. There, over eighteen months, he undertook his famous experiments on the carcasses of horses, the result of which was the book *The Anatomy of the Horse*. His reputation for buying any and every dead horse in the locality was legendary. He constructed supports so that the animal could be arranged in any pose. Stubbs was one of those who never received his due from the Royal Academy, always regarded as a 'horse painter' and therefore working in an inferior genre. In recent years Stubbs has been re-assessed and his stature has grown to the measure of the greatest English artists. His was a brilliant skill in composition and life-like rendering, reminiscent of the quattrocento, and his knowledge and sheer originality unsurpassed.

Yet Stubbs also came to the northern Wolds of Lincolnshire in search of patronage and he set to painting the local gentry, in portraiture and in their carriages and on horseback. One lovely painting in particular shows his fine observation of landscape, that of Sir John Nelthorpe on foot with his dogs Hector and Tinker shooting over Barton Field. A wide vista of the flat agricultural land of the Wolds tops gives distant views of the two churches close together in Barton on Humber.

Patronage has always been important in stimulating artistic and literary endeavour, and the Wolds has had only a few wealthy landowners. The Yarborough estate around Brocklesby is distinguished by its woodlands and shelter belts of trees. Creating such landscapes and rendering them in paint was a favourite activity of the landed and wealthy, but the utilitarian love of land that produces good harvests is well expressed by one of Virginia Woolf's characters, Ralph Denman, in *Night and Day* (1919), when he says of Lincolnshire, 'Real country. No gentleman's seats.' It might well have been spoken of the Wolds with its comparatively few great houses.

Two figures stand out in the story of the artistic and literary heritage of the Wolds – Peter DeWint and Alfred Tennyson, and in their creative work can be seen much of the great attraction that the Wolds holds for people today. DeWint was born in 1784 at Stone near Hanley in Staffordshire. His father was from a wealthy Dutch family who settled in New England. In 1802 he moved to London in pursuit of his artistic training and met William Hilton whose father, also William, was a portrait painter from Newark who later moved to Lincoln. It was in London that he was inspired by the drawings and watercolours of Thomas Girtin (1775–1802), the tragically short-lived, brilliant and influential watercolourist of whom Turner is reported to have said (probably apocryphally), 'If Girtin had lived, I should have starved.' Eclipsed by the great achievements of his long-lived contemporary, Girtin's influence has recently been re-appraised. This influence on DeWint may be seen in his predilection for great views over vast flat vistas commanded from some prominence, as in the 'Lincolnshire Cornfield near Horncastle', and a particularly fine untitled picture, which might indeed be of the Lincolnshire Wolds, in the British Museum, 'Panoramic Landscape – 1820'. This, it should also be said, was a particularly Dutch tradition, which may also have influenced his work.

It was in 1806 that DeWint first visited Lincoln and fell in love with Hilton's younger sister Harriet whom he married in 1810. In 1807 his father died and his elder brother proved ineffectual in providing for the family, the responsibility falling on Peter, an important factor in driving forward his artistic career. In 1814 he bought a house with Hilton in Lincoln, but continued to move between his home in London and the house in Drury Lane. DeWint never lived in Lincoln for any length of time, travelling greatly, and amassing a great body of work, much of which was discovered after his death in 1849 in his attic in London. Many of these were oils and together with his watercolours they are justly regarded as the work of one of the finest English landscape painters.

Baudelaire observed: *Romanticism is precisely situated neither in choice of subjects nor in exact truth, but in a mode of feeling.* This feeling became a way of self-knowing, a revelatory relationship. It was a counterpoint to the Age of Reason, to the building intensity of the Industrial Revolution, and in rural unrest as well, and found its finest form in the literary and artistic works of the eighteenth and nineteenth centuries in the expression of landscape. In DeWint the strength of feeling in the landscape is most vividly evoked and born of a personal relationship. The landscape in oils, 'Lincolnshire Cornfield near Horncastle', captures a sublime tranquillity that looks outwards from the

FIGURE 54. A harvesting scene on the open flat-topped central Wolds west of Louth by Peter DeWint (1784–1849). LOUTH MUSEUM

Wolds – one of its most important atmospheric characteristics. John Clare wrote a sonnet to him, including the lines

> *…Yet in thy landscapes I can well descry*
> *Thy breathing hues as nature's counterpart*
> *No painted freaks – no wild romantic sky*
> *No rocks or mountains as the rich sublime*
> *Hath made thee famous but the sunny truth*
> *Of nature that doth mark thee for all time…*

The experience of nature infused the works of Alfred Tennyson (1809–1892). In 1850, the year *In Memoriam* was published, he was appointed Poet Laureate in succession to William Wordsworth and his fame was firmly established. His burial in Westminster Abbey was accompanied by an outpouring of national mourning. T. S. Eliot said that Tennyson *has the finest ear of any English poet since Milton*. Born within the Wolds at Somersby where his father was Rector, he spent much of his time until he was 28 walking the lanes and byways of the Wolds. In his writings there are many direct and indirect allusions to those early experiences. Peter Levi in his biography of Tennyson says of them: *…his poetry…is often deeply infused with memories of his childhood. The woods where there is a holy well are still full of snowdrops in season, another wood a mile or so away has a wonderful crop of orchids, the landscape is still agricultural, and Somersby is still deeply lost on the edge of nowhere.*

It was a changing landscape then, as now, as rural quiet gave way to steam engines and machinery. Artists sought out the remaining wild places, yet Tennyson really experienced what he wrote about. A nature-poem *Ode to Memory*, written in boyhood, speaks from knowledge

> *…bleat*
> *Of the thick-fleeced sheep from wattled folds,*
> *Upon the ridged wolds,*
> *When the first matin-song hath waken'd loud*
> *Over the dark dewy earth forlorn,*
> *What time the amber morn*
> *Forth gushes from beneath a low-hung cloud.*

Tennyson's mature work in *In Memoriam A. H. H.* describes both the detail of the intimate seclusion and also the grand open spaces:

> *Calm and deep peace on this high wold,*
> *And on these dews that drench the furze,*
> *And all the silvery gossamers*
> *That twinkle into green and gold:*
>
> *Calm and still light on yon great plain*
> *That sweeps with all its autumn bowers,*
> *And crowded farms and lessening towers,*
> *To mingle with the bounding main:*

Again, another familiar experience to those who know the hills and valleys of the Wolds appears in *The Lady of Shalott*:

> *On either side the river lie*
> *Long fields of barley and of rye,*
> *That clothe the wold and meet the sky;*
> *And thro' the field the road runs by*
> *To many-tower'd Camelot;*

Whilst both DeWint and Tennyson enjoyed the views outward that the Wolds afford across distant horizons to vale and sea, Tennyson also understood the intimacy and detail of the landscape picturesquely seen in the well known lines from *Maud*, inspired by Rosa Baring and her home at Harrington, an impressive house only a couple of miles from Somersby:

> *Come into the garden, Maud,*
> *I am here at the gate alone;*
> *And the woodbine spices are wafted abroad,*
> *And the musk of the rose is blown.*

And most charmingly this is seen in *The Brook*, which Tennyson described as the sum of all the many brooks, but reminiscent of a favourite childhood place of his and his brothers:

> *By thirty hills I hurry down,*
> *Or slip between the ridges,*
> *By twenty thorpes, a little town,*
> *And half a hundred bridges.*

FIGURE 55. William Brown's Panorama of Louth (1844–47): the right panel with a 180 degrees view of the Wolds.

Till last by Philip's farm I flow
To join the brimming river,
For men may come and men may go,
But I go on for ever.

There are many worthy artistic depictions of the Wolds landscapes, some topographical and some picturesque, but an unusual and indeed extraordinary depiction of the Wolds comes from the huge 'Panorama of Louth'. It was painted by William Brown, a local Methodist, housepainter and newspaper reporter, drawn in 1844 from the top of the spire of St James's church, which at 295 feet is the tallest parish spire in England when it was scaffolded for repair work. It was first exhibited in 1847 in Louth Mansion House. Regarded as 'a major work of nineteenth century provincial art' the Panorama is reminiscent of Girtin's amazing and now lost panoramic project for London from the Thames, the 'Eidometropolis' conceived in 1801. The very word 'panorama' was a neologism coined in 1791 from the Greek, meaning 'view of all', by the inventor Robert Barker who had patented the idea of creating 360 degree views, 'to make observers…feel as if really on the spot', at which he was remarkably successful. Brown's two panel 'Panorama' was intended to be flat and not curved, in all eighteen feet long, a veritable tour de force of the art of illusion – the depiction of curved space on a flat surface! Full of the most valuable and accurate historical detail, the bright prospect with light greens and bright red ochres, reminiscent of Italy, gives an altogether pleasing and airy vista of town, wolds, marshland, sea and sky. Closer examination towards the rising ground of the Wolds reveals in painstaking detail a rich agricultural landscape, but historically a comparatively recent representation of enclosure fields with new smaller and younger hedges. The really astonishing thing is that the visitor to Louth arriving over the Wolds sees the town emerge from a fold of the hills signposted by its graceful parish spire. The view from the town does not afford a clear view uphill, but from the great spire of St James's Brown captured a rare spectacle.

The explosion in personal mobility in the twentieth century has brought many more visitors to the Wolds, and to guide them many words have been written to describe the scenery and help the visitor to interpret what they are looking at. This twist in the story of the romantic consumption of landscape is accompanied by a new awareness of the value of landscape for itself, sometimes described as the 'sense of place' or 'poetry of place', and took shape in the designation of parks and areas of specialness.

A visit to some parts of the Wolds in the early 1950s would have lulled the visitor into believing that little had changed since Tennyson's time, but even as Brown's 'Panorama' demonstrates how change was reshaping the landscape before their very eyes, so the land and the people were undergoing a further post-war revolution – from which we have not yet emerged. Even as the visitors were arriving in larger numbers, the first phase – what might be called 'feeding the nation', was underway. In the early 1970s this gave way to a second phase when ecological considerations came back into view, previously obscured by the drive for efficiency and productivity. Then the costs of the Common Agricultural Policy were beginning to spiral and so began the first of many attempts by stick and carrot to support and direct farming – a third phase. The landscape of the Wolds is at the mercy of forces outside the control of its inhabitants, and more recently with the globalisation of the market place, and crises such as foot and mouth disease, our control over the development of landscape values seems to be even more tenuous. It is against this commercial backdrop that an artistic renaissance has taken place with more artists, possibly than ever before, interpreting the varieties of Wolds landscapes. Inspired by such artists as Ivon Hitchins, Graham Sutherland, Ben Nicholson, Paul Nash and Christopher Wood, many fine artists have been finding rich subject matter. To mention but a few, Tom Brooker, David Cuppleditch, Tony Bartl, David Morris, Eric Littlewood, Keith Roper and David Tarttelin give a variety of interpretations, still in the picturesque tradition that links them to the Romantic vision.

At the same time new literary appraisals have blossomed. Of particular note is the 1990 Booker Prize winning novel *Possession* by A. S. Byatt, released as a motion picture starring Gwyneth Paltrow in 2002. A. S. Byatt and her sister Margaret Drabble, also a fine novelist, grew up in Sheffield, and have longstanding Lincolnshire connections. Her description of the Wolds must be one of the most revealing ever written. Dr Maud Bailey is taking Roland to Seal Court, a rambling decrepit house which may hold the secret of their researches. She says:

FIGURE 56. Winter on the Wolds near Stenigot by Tom Brooker.
DAVID ROBINSON COLLECTION

The wolds of Lincolnshire are a small surprise. Tennyson grew up in one of their twisting valleys. From them he made the cornfields of immortal Camelot…They drove over the plain, up the rolling road out of the valley. The valleys are deep and narrow, some wooded, some grassy, some ploughed. The ridges run sharply across the sky, always bare, some ploughed. The rest of the county is marsh or fen or flat farmed plain. These slightly rolling hills appear to be folded out of the surface of the earth, but that is not the case; they are part of a dissected tableland. The villages are buried in the valleys, at the end of blind funnels.

Poetry too has blossomed with encouragement and support in this new awareness of the 'distinctiveness of place', the *genius loci* Robert Etty, a native poet of the Wolds, has the ability to get *inside* an experience of place. His poem, *Orange Tips* is evocative of the Wolds:

> *High on the dirt road beyond*
> *Pepper's Holt the valley of beans*
> *Has a violet tinge, but close-up*
> *Each stalk looks as if butterflies are clustering in twenties*
> *And thirties and testing the wind*
> *With white wings. From nests*
> *Inside blown tufts of corn*
> *Larks scale ledges of the sky.*
> *Further over a chalky rim,*
> *A lapwing waves like a glove.*
>
> *Two orange-tips almost alight on*
> *May blossom that dazzles us*

On the Aswardby road, but flitter
Instead over buttercup fields and
Chewing bullocks' backs.

I hope
As we clamber the dock-leafy
Plough-track that Helen might
Sometime remember this minute:
Hill, the horizons, the colours
Of beans; following orange-
Tips, disappearing.

The Wolds have a rich legacy of religious buildings, which are in themselves, in stone and decoration, subtle footnotes to the genius of place. The flowering in stone and stained glass, wood and metal are a paean of praise, raising earth in the worship of the Creator, the 'elevation of geology' into vernacular buildings. Once again patronage has played a key part paying for the beautification of God's house, but in recent times the democratization of religious life has led some congregations, inspired by local distinctiveness, to commission new expressions and celebrations, a spate of which greeted the new millennium. New stained glass is a favourite choice with many churches having plain glass, the result of earlier political and religious upheaval. One piece of note is by Glenn Carter in St Mary, Rothwell. The Joseph Nickerson window, in memory of the pioneering plant breeder, is powerfully evocative of the Wolds, full of life and movement, wild birds and game birds, hares and wheat, science and landscape.

A new art of place in the late twentieth and early twenty-first centuries, with roots more in post-modernist philosophy than the Romantic spirit, has also been revealing new qualities – often a sense of the transitory nature of reality. Janette Porter, a land artist, has undertaken a number of land-based projects around the county, where poetry and sculpture, land forms, history and agricultural practice flow together. On the Wolds near Raithby, between 1997 and 1999, she created three living sculptures from farmland plants, the *Living Earth Sculptures*. Each work involved a long preparation with local people and children from nearby schools, and numerous events and celebrations surrounded the whole process.

Mike Clarke, a potter from Fulbeck, and his daughter Harriet, a photography graduate from Cardiff, became Millennium Artists and undertook an unusual project across the county to document the passage of people through place. Three of these took place in churches in the Wolds, at St Olave, Ruckland, St Margaret, Bag Enderby and St Mary, Tetford. Harriet pioneered the use of a pinhole camera with very long exposures to chart the ghostly passage of people through the church, and these were combined with Mike's clay casts of floors and thresholds.

These unusual works, with new perspectives, indicate novel ways to explore our relationship with the sense of place. Other artists are inspired in more

FIGURE 58. Lincoln Cathedral punctuates the western horizon from Flint Hill by Tom Brooker.

abstract ways by shapes and forms, experiences and reflections to create patterns and textures in multiple media that inform our sensual awareness. We live in the age of the photographic image, and the subtle power of the image to play on our feelings is well explored. The Wolds is a rich ground for the image, with a number of books of old photographs having been produced, but new and powerful images, such as the colour photographs in Janet and Peter Roworth's *Lincolnshire Moods*, are communicating the genius of the Wolds to a new generation.

Henry Winn

Henry Winn (1816–1914) was many things to the people of Fulletby – shoemaker, grocer, draper, general dealer, paperhanger, surveyor, tax collector, census enumerator, constable, sick club visitor, Sunday School superintendent and schoolmaster. He was also a man of words, regularly writing in clear copperplate in many volumes of feint-ruled notebooks sat at his high shop desk. Writing was his life-long hobby, collecting and noting both local and wider history and contributing articles to newspapers and magazines on a wide variety of topics including Lincolnshire celebrities and curiosities, skits and proverbs – and a constant stream of poetry, some of which he had printed on his tea-wrappers.

> The highest art that man on earth can reach
> Is rightly to employ the part of speech.
> The greatest power the world has ever known
> ….
>
> Is words – so easy formed and glibly spoken,
> So wild and wayward when their checks are broken
> ….
>
> 'Tis with the pen the mighty mind records
> Its flights and fancies in the form of words.
> This sage advice I give to old and young,
> Guard well the flow of words from pen and tongue.

And so he did, and in doing so he left among his poems graphic accounts of the Battle of Winceby and a record of the 'Druid Stone' there; an account of the 'bold activity' of How (or Hoe) Hill, the natural feature near Fulletby; and a description of a wild glen at Fulletby called Pot and Pan:

> Three cloven hills a tiny stream divides,
> Rough brush and bracken hide their rugged sides.
> Two gushing fountains from two little rills,
> Winding their devious course among the hills;
> Their banks with ferns of various sorts abound;
> Foxgloves and bluebells beautify the ground;
> And in the sheltered nooks and shady grot,
> Spring up primrose and forget-me-not.

Henry Winn
LINCOLNSHIRE WOLDS COUNTRYSIDE SERVICE

In similar simple vein he described his Native Place:

> How lovely are the healthy breezy Wolds,
> Fair Lindsey's chalky mountains, which extend
> From Horncastle northward to the Humber;
> Among whose sheltering hill is found
> Rich valleys, quiet nooks, and sheltered dells,
> Where nestle down beside their fertile farms
> The scanty population of the land.

Another poem enumerates the goods he sold in his front room shop – an astonishing list which would surely supply the wants of any of the villagers:

> Gingers, pimentos, peppers, muscatelles,
> Raisins and currants, candy-peel and spice,
> Oatmeal and sago, barley, groats and rice,
> Cake-seeds and cocoa, treacle, butter, cheese,
> Eggs, bacon, lard, tobacco, sugar, pease.
> Rich flavour'd teas, that can't be beat by Rose,
> and coffee, strong as Cassell every shows.
>
> Dresses for ladies, cashmere or delain;
> Ribbands and gloves, both fancy goods and plain;
> Aprons and handkerchiefs, collars and shawls;
> Prints, calicos, and cotton-reels and balls;
> Embossed linings, holland, cord, and jean;
> Roll jaconets, and muslins – checked and plain.
>
> Gunpowder, caps and shot, steel-pens and quills,
> Essence and opiates, spirits, tinctures, pills;
> Nails of all sorts, pins, needles, knives and combs;
> Earthenware, besoms, mops, mop-shafts, and brooms;
> Red orchre, pitch and rosin, starch and blue;
> All kinds of brushes, blacking, ink and glue;
> Locks, bolts and gimlets, shovels, spades and files.
>
> Danzig black beer, French vinegar and oils,
> Envelopes, wafers, sealing wax, and papers;
> Apples and pears, figs, biscuits, nuts and capers;
> Lard, whipcord, ploughlines, holland, twine and traces;
> Epsom salts, bear's grease, blister salve, and braces.

It is through such a word record that we are able to gain an insight of life in a nineteenth-century Wolds village.

David Robinson

CHAPTER TEN

Changes on the Farm

David Hill

The impact of the agricultural revolution of the second half of the twentieth century on the farming landscape of the Wolds was probably greater than that of the enclosure of open fields and warrens and introduction of four course crop rotation and livestock breeding two centuries before. At the beginning of the Second World War farming had barely recovered from the depression of the 1920s and 1930s, and the country was over dependent on imported food. Merchant shipping was threatened by enemy action, and home food production became a paramount objective. War Agricultural Committees were established with sweeping powers to direct growing particular crops and to allocate scarce machinery. Male labour was called up for the armed services and the agricultural workforce was supplemented by the Women's Land Army. The potential for food production on the Wolds had to be maximised.

With the return of peace, agriculture was very much controlled by government agencies, a recognition of the importance of the industry. However, farming methods had changed little and most of the work still involved manual labour. The purpose of the 1947 Agriculture Act was to increase home food production, with farm prices reviewed annually and set at a level to enable profitable production. Farm technology was changing with more tractors available, but the binder and thrashing drum were still the main harvesting tools, manure was hand-loaded and spread and hay was still carted loose. Wolds farms were larger than average and fields larger, but the chalk soil was thin. Cropping was largely barley, and sheep still played an important role in getting fertility back into the soil.

However, science had begun a process of change which would accelerate rapidly. The key developments in the 1950s were the introduction of the combine harvester and the development of crop spraying to control weeds. Early machines were unsophisticated by modern standards, but they eliminated the labour intensive tasks of binding, stooking, leading, stacking and thrashing. Then came the baler to pick up the discarded straw and turn it into neat bales. The baler also changed the laborious work of haymaking. Labourers began to leave the land as their jobs became redundant.

The crop sprayer of the 1950s was a crude tool. It applied a mixture of chemicals with a modest degree of control, but the impact was dramatic. Fields with red poppies once distinguished many parts of the Wolds. The soil was, and still is impregnated with the seed of generations of poppies waiting their

FIGURE 59. Combine
harvesting.
DERRICK FURLONG

chance to bloom. Early spray chemicals took away the splashes of rich red, and
the yellow charlock (generally known as ketlocks), together with thistles and
many of the once common cornfield weeds.

Rabbits were once a profitable crop on the Wolds, kept in extensive warrens,
with hay and roots grown for their winter feed. However, after the warrens were
ploughed up, rabbits were a constant plague on the fresh shoots of corn and
other crops. Some families, the Dixons of Swaby for example, made a living
as rabbit catchers and selling them at local markets. Then the advent of the
myxomatosis disease in the late 1950s decimated the rabbit population and crop
output increased dramatically.

Under a new Agriculture Act in 1957 the annual price review awards were
limited to that part of farm production deemed to be in the national interest.
This meant prices were reduced by an arbitrary amount to allow for increased
efficiency. In other words farmers were under pressure to increase production
or reduce costs. Small units were squeezed and farm sizes expanded still
further. Through the next decade those pressures increased, and so did farm
production.

The labour force shrank as more machinery was employed and the government
Advisory Service actively encouraged change on the farm. Grants were available
to improve farm buildings and a new generation of combine harvesters, linked
to bulk drying and storage of grain on the farm, rapidly increased the productive
capacity of the Wolds, where cereal farming became the most profitable option.
Indeed, farmers were advised to cease their livestock enterprise, particularly
cattle, and concentrate on crops. There was also a decline in numbers of sheep,
the care of which was more labour intensive and therefore did not fit into the
new concept of low cost and streamlined production. Whereas a few years
back an individual farm might have produced a numerous and wide range of

individual products, now farms were concentrating on producing just a handful of different crops.

Amid these changes, rabbits made a comeback, having built up some immunity to myxomatosis. Government encouraged the formation of rabbit clearance societies where groups of farmers undertook to try to control rabbits, and wood pigeons and rooks, with subsidised cyanide gas for rabbits and cheap cartridges. It made little real difference and government support was withdrawn.

New crops made an appearance, particularly peas. The fishing and freezing industry in Grimsby spawned a sizeable market for frozen vegetables. As fishing declined in the 1960s, frozen foods expanded, and a number of Wolds farms within range of Grimsby started contract-growing of fresh peas. At first the harvested plants were taken to a static pea-viner on the farm which shook the peas from the pods before rapid transport to the factory for washing and freezing. Later mobile viners carried out the process in the field. With the technology developed the crop was easy to grow, there was over production and the price fell.

The Wolds was never noted for vegetable production, but casual crops of cabbage, swedes and turnip were grown. There was however, a period when

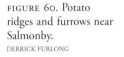

FIGURE 60. Potato ridges and furrows near Salmonby.
DERRICK FURLONG

brussel sprouts were an important crop on some lands, based, as with peas, on the frozen food market. Potatoes were grown for a time on the fen-edge sandstone Wolds, and there was an unusual experiment with daffodils and tulips at Scamblesby.

Relentless pressure for more efficient farming continued into the 1970s, with a new consideration looming, that of membership of the European Economic Community (EEC). The average Wolds farm was bigger and more efficient than most British farms and had little to fear from the prospect of change to a European support system – the Common Agricultural Policy (CAP). This had started in the 1960s and was intended to raise the standard of income on farms to that of urban areas. The British system of supporting farm income was by direct subsidies, allowing crops to be sold at market prices, often below the cost of production. The CAP system was to impose a tariff wall with the price at the farm gate high enough to cover production costs and a reasonable profit.

Throughout those years the pattern of farming on the Wolds continued the process of change. Farms grew in size and declined in number, and livestock was reduced with more concentration on cereal production. Combine harvesters got bigger and more efficient, and tractors more sophisticated. Perhaps more importantly seed breeders developed new and more productive varieties. The Wolds produced their own breeding company, Nickersons of Rothwell where local farmer and businessman, Joe Nickerson, later Sir Joseph, introduced many new varieties. The objective was always to introduce crops with a wide market but the special interests and needs of the home farm were kept in mind. Coupled with more advanced chemical fertilizers and sprays, output per acre increased.

FIGURE 61. Oilseed rape.
DERRICK FURLONG

FIGURE 62. Borage.
DERRICK FURLONG

FIGURE 63. Linseed.
LINCOLNSHIRE WOLDS
COUNTRYSIDE SERVICE

Entry into the EEC in the early 1970s allayed farmers' fears of reduced income, but the financing mechanism, the green pound, almost invariably resulted in British farmers receiving around a quarter less than their continental counterparts. However, some benefits did emerge, easily seen in the new crop colours on the Wolds. Oilseed rape had been grown since the Middle Ages for lamp oil, but now there was pressure to grow it as a main crop because of shortage of vegetable oils. Large fields of brilliant yellow lit up the Wolds

FIGURE 64. Baling hay
the modern way.
DERRICK FURLONG

FIGURE 65. Harvesting
sugar beet.
DERRICK FURLONG

in a way no other crop had done. Oilseed rape also proved an excellent break
crop: a rotation of rape, wheat, wheat and barley gave few harvesting problems,
and reduced further the need for livestock to provide rotational fertility. Then
blue was added with the introduction of linseed to meet the needs of paint
manufacture, and now there is another hue with borage.

Another visual change became apparent in the 1980s – the 'tramlines' in
cereal fields. By omitting to sow two rows spaced at intervals when drilling, the
tramlines could be used by machinery spreading fertilizer and crop spraying.

FIGURE 66. Lincoln Red
cattle.

It had been customary to have some autumn and some spring sown cereals; autumn sowing gave a longer growing period and higher yields, but the crop was subject to fungal diseases and could be damaged by severe weather. The new more precise crop management enabled chemical control, so autumn sowing became the norm and yields increased again.

The Wolds now had a green cover for most of the winter, and the traditional spring barley, sought by the malting trade and a main crop on Wolds farms, diminished. Moreover, with the greater demand for lager beers, requirement for the traditional product declined, and the malt kiln in Louth is now closed and facing imminent demolition. Another benefit of having less bare land was a lower risk of nitrates leaching from the soil into water supplies in the winter.

The increased capacity to produce cereals, particularly wheat, meant an opportunity for export, in which the Wolds played a part because of proximity to Gainsborough on the Trent and Grimsby and Immingham on the Humber. In fact the export trade became an important outlet for grain from the Wolds, with the ability to supply large quantities of wheat, and barley, to required standards and within strict time schedules.

Under the European tariff system, surplus production was taken off the market and stored for sale in a period of shortage. The mid 1980s were highly productive years, resulting in grain 'mountains', often stored in old aircraft hangars, and by the early 1990s it was clear that some new control of production was required. That was set-aside, where farmers were required to leave some land uncultivated, and be compensated for doing so. Poor weather and low productive seasons also reduced the problem.

FIGURE 67. Louth
livestock market.
DERRICK FURLONG

Set-aside reduced the intensity of farming and provided opportunities for conservation measures. At first it was for only one year, or on margins of fields, but some in long term set-aside reverted to a more natural state to the benefit of wildlife. The advent of set-aside also stimulated alternative uses of land including recreation and green tourism. And as fossil fuels become scarcer, there may be potential to grow energy crops.

Already, in the early years of the twenty-first century, Lincolnshire is being referred to as the 'fuel basket' of the country as well as the 'bread basket'. The potential and the technology is there, and oil seeds are being converted to fuel to supplement carbon fuels, and even to power vehicles solely on such oil. Small plants for farms to produce the fuel for their own vehicles are now possible, mirroring the horse age when the motivating power for the farm fed on the grass without the need for outside supplies. Cereal crops and sugar beet offer scope for conversion to ethanol, and although growing crops requires inputs of fertilizer and fuel for tractors, currently mainly based on carbon fuels, there is a significant energy gain in the process. Political will and pricing remain as obstacles but as we use up the carbon resources of the world the pressures will increase. As always the Wolds will be a major part of any changes.

Throughout this period the farmstead has adapted to meet the new and varied demands. At first the old traditional brick farming range, with the crewyards, barns, cartsheds and small buildings were adapted. With the move to bulk grain handling, and with the government incentives new specialized buildings were erected, and gradually the picture changed. Today the large multi-purpose building is the norm. Farm security and the protection of valuable assets

FIGURE 68. Thin chalk
soils on what was reputed
to be the largest field on
the Wolds at Withcall.
DAVID ROBINSON

requires most farm equipment to be locked up in buildings when not in use.
The modern on-farm grain store is frequently a large building with clear floor
space where the grain can be deposited in heaps, leaving the building available
for other uses when the grain has been sold. Where livestock are kept they are
housed in purpose built units to provide easy management. Today, those old
brick buildings, once so much part of the visual impact of the Wolds, are likely
to be adapted for other uses. Small factory units for domestic use can be found
where the structure and location make that appropriate. The new buildings,
whilst large and arguably less pleasing on the eye, are mostly hidden in the
rolling landscape, with effort made to avoid them being obtrusive.

The natural landscapes of the Wolds have been shaped and reshaped by those
who live there and work on the land. Trees have been planted to provide coverts
for hunting and to protect game. Trees have been removed to accommodate
modern farming. Trees, like people, have a limited life span, and the agricultural
depressions of the 1920s and 1930s followed by the war period meant that for
almost half a century little work was done to maintain and improve the stock
of trees on farms. In the last twenty-five years these changes appear to have
slowed. Extensive planting of trees has occurred, with some notable examples
at Stenigot and at South Ormsby. Hedges that came with the enclosures have
been removed to make appropriate field sizes for modern farming. Today we
are seeing new hedge planting, encouraged by the government's environmental
policies, which bodes well for the future.

A mere 60 years ago it was beyond imagining that the farmland of the Wolds
would become so productive and surplus grain a problem to the extent that land
would be taken out of cultivation. That evolution of farming, driven by need,
economics and politics, seemed more like a revolution. In the last few years
farming has again seen a period of major change. Profitability has declined. Few

farms can afford to maintain a significant labour force and individual farmers are doing the manual work single-handed on what were once 'large farms'. People are becoming more aware of the needs and problems of farming, and more aware that their own food can and arguably should be locally produced. Change is on-going, quiet revolution following quiet revolution, yet it is surprising how relatively little the overall appearance of the Wolds has changed.

Fowler of Louth

'By Fowler of Louth' is a familiar phrase in publications about Lincolnshire churches, but his name was known outside the county and he also designed different secular buildings. James Fowler was born at Lichfield in December 1828, trained as a lithographic artist and produced plates of ecclesiastical buildings for publication. In 1849, at the age of 20, he arrived in Louth to do work on the House of Correction. Two years later he went into partnership with Joseph Maughan, lithographer and surveyor.

As well as coastal surveys, they published measured drawings of the tower and spire of St James's church, Louth. Fowler became interested in church restoration and he joined the Architectural Society for the Diocese of Lincoln. In designing new churches, the first of which was East Ravendale St Martin in 1857, and in the restoring of others, he was driven by the promptings of the Ecclesiological Society.

His career blossomed in the mid-1850s, and within five years he had built a hall (Dalby in the southern Wolds), Horncastle Corn Exchange, three schools, ten parsonages, three chapels, and a new church and restored eight others. He established his own architectural practice and in the 1860s was involved with 79 buildings, 42 of them new ones including 15 parsonages, 12 churches, seven schools and two almshouses. The next decade was even busier with no less than 89 buildings ranging from new London churches to Lincolnshire farm labourers' houses, and the Louth Waterworks at Hubbard's Hills. He was also made the Lincoln Diocesan Surveyor, and found time to be elected onto Louth Borough Council, serving twice as Mayor.

St Mary and Gabriel, Binbrook, designed by James Fowler and built of ironstone.
LINCOLNSHIRE WOLDS COUNTRYSIDE SERVICE

His output in 38 years of architectural practice was prodigious, much of it condensed into 20 years. Over 240 buildings he designed or restored have been traced: 27 new churches including four in London, 43 parsonages, 13 schools, four almshouses and a convalescent home, and over a hundred churches restored or rebuilt. In addition there were private houses and commercial properties including banks, offices and shops. Of all of these, some 60 were in the Wolds.

He handled the bulk of the work himself, and did not take on a pupil or assistant until 1869. During the busy 1870s he had two assistants and two pupils, including J. J. Cresswell who later designed the original Louth Museum (1910). Fowler's son Reginald joined the practice in 1882 and continued for a short time after his father's death.

In public service, Fowler was Mayor of Louth five times, a record never surpassed. The impartiality and dignity he brought to the office commanded the respect of all, and he was President or Secretary of many organisations in the town. When he was Mayor during Queen Victoria's Golden Jubilee year he designed and presented to the town a ceremonial mace.

His health began failing from 1888 although he continued to be involved in public affairs. Following a severe chill he died on 10 October 1892, aged 63.

There is a display about James Fowler and his work in Louth Museum.

David Robinson

CHAPTER ELEVEN

Restoring Biodiversity

Ted Smith

The vegetation of the Wolds has been largely determined for more than five thousand years by man's use of the land. The first farming peoples of the Neolithic and the Bronze Age began the clearance of the original cover of light woodland and scrub for crop cultivation and grazing by animals. During periods of low farming activity scrub would be quick to return, but from the early Middle Ages the demand for wool ensured that vast areas of grassland were maintained by sheep. As sheep numbers declined after the seventeenth century, rabbit grazing ensured the survival of large expanses of short turf.

FIGURE 69. Restoration of arable to downland as an extension to the Red Hill nature reserve was assisted by grazing with Hebridean sheep.
HARRY TURNER

Chalk Grasslands

Much of the chalk is covered by thin boulder clay and other glacial deposits, but on the exposed plateaux, and the brows of hillsides, grazing maintained a short downland turf with a rich assemblage of lime-loving grasses and other

plants. Among those were thyme, milkwort, rockrose, salad burnet, bird's-foot trefoil, purging flax, hairy violet, quaking grass, felwort, pyramidal, bee and other orchids, yellow-wort, scabious and knapweed. These are all plants adapted to growing in pervious, quick draining soil and in situations fully exposed to the desiccating effects of sun and wind. Many are deeply rooted; most are low-growing or mat-forming. To minimise water loss some, like purging flax and milkwort, have small leaves; others like felwort, yellow-wort and orchids have thick cuticles, whilst others like hairy violet and wild basil have a coating of hairs.

FIGURE 70. Flowers of the Wolds by Mary Smith.

FIGURE 71. Silverines Meadow nature reserve near Goulceby with a wonderful display of meadow saxifrage.
TED SMITH

The vast expanses of grassland supported a great variety of birds, insects and other animals. Great bustard and stone curlew both nested, and there were lapwings, wheatears, sky larks and meadow pipits. Buzzards and red kites and other raptors from nearby wooded areas hunted over the open ground. Butterflies too would have been in abundance: common grassland species including common blue and brown argus, and some like marbled white and dark green fritillary which have subsequently disappeared from the Wolds.

The decline of the woollen industry, followed in the eighteenth century by the technical and economic revolution in English agriculture, spelt the end of the Wold downs and sheep-walks. Change was remarkably rapid. When Arthur Young came to Lincolnshire to make his report for the Board of Agriculture in 1799 there were still some extensive tracts of open sheep-walks and rabbit warrens, but much enclosure and ploughing had taken place since his previous visit 30 years earlier and 'improvement' was proceeding apace. Within another 30 years the transformation was complete. William Cobbett in 1830 saw only 'a very fine corn country' … 'the hills not downs as in Wiltshire, but cultivated all over'. And J. A. Clarke writing in 1851 remarked that 'no portion of the ground has been allowed to remain (as on the Downs of southern England) a tract of sheep-walks in its primitive vegetation of heath and fern, but the highest parts are all in tillage and the whole length of the Wolds is intersected by neat whitethorn hedges, the solitary furze bush appearing only where a roadside or plantation offers an uncultivated space'.

There was indeed little left of the plant-rich chalk grassland. It survived only in tiny patches on steep hillsides, roadside verges and in a few disused quarries. In the agricultural intensification of the second half of the last century even some of those patches disappeared or deteriorated through further cultivation, cessation of grazing and, in the case of quarries, infilling with refuse. Recent surveys have revealed less than 50 hectares of the habitat in the Wolds.

Its high biodiversity and relative scarcity in Britain and in Europe makes calcareous grassland a habitat of significant conservation value, and the Lincolnshire Biodiversity Action Plan set targets for maintaining, safeguarding and improving existing areas, and recreating 100 hectares of chalk and limestone grassland in the county. Much is already being done to achieve those targets. Seven calcareous grassland sites in the Wolds covering 24 hectares are designated Sites of Special Scientific Interest (SSSI) and four of those covering 16 hectares are nature reserves managed by the Lincolnshire Wildlife Trust. Notable among them is the Red Hill at Goulceby where the red chalk is exposed in the hillside cliff. This is one of the richest fragments of grassland in the Wolds. Most of the characteristic flowers of the chalk are there together with a variety of butterflies, moths and other insects. In 1998 the Trust acquired 23 hectares of adjoining former arable land which has been restored to sheep-grazed grassland. Skylarks and meadow pipits nest there, and common buzzards, which have returned to the Wolds after an absence of nearly 150 years, are frequently seen. This is the largest restoration project so far undertaken in the Wolds, but smaller areas are being restored elsewhere through Environmental Stewardship Schemes. Other patches of calcareous grassland occur in Irby Dale and Swallow Wold in the north, and at Oxcombe, Swaby and Skendleby Psalter valleys in the south.

Chalk Pits

Disused chalk pits soon develop a typical chalk flora, but tend to become dominated by scrub unless appropriately managed. The Wildlife Trust has three such reserves on the eastern edge of the Wolds at Candlesby Hill, Claxby and Little Cawthorpe. These are quiet, intimate places with a wealth of flowers, not least the orchids – twayblade, common spotted, pyramidal and the compellingly beautiful bee orchid. They are places too for butterflies and bees and for birds. Whitethroat and blackcap nest in the scrub, and in shadier places spotted flycatchers snap up insects. Linnets and goldfinches are attracted by the abundance of seeds. Old chalk pits are important wildlife 'refuges' and 'reservoirs' in a countryside with few wild places. In addition to that, they provide valuable exposures of the chalk which help to unravel the geological history of the Wolds.

They have much human interest too. For several centuries they supplied stone for the Marsh roads, and old lime kilns – which the Trust is carefully

preserving at Candlesby Hill and Claxby – are relics of a nineteenth-century industrial process, small-scale but important for local agriculture. Claxby also has its mill mound which was originally a Bronze Age round barrow, and the remains of the village smithy near the entrance. These are places where man and nature have interacted over several centuries. Now the Trust's management is designed to retain the various stages of vegetation succession from open ground to woodland.

Road Verges

Enclosure destroyed the open downland, but it left many wide road verges, some of them beside Roman roads, prehistoric trackways and old drove roads. Whatever their original purpose – for common grazing, for droving or simply to leave adequate width for traffic in the days before hardcore roads – these strips of wayside grassland have retained many of the colourful and well-loved flowers of the chalk hills and constitute an important widespread wildlife resource in intensively cultivated countryside. In addition to the commoner plants, several species which are localized or even rare in Lincolnshire occur on verges. They also provide a refuge for grassland butterflies and for small mammals which attract hunting kestrels and barn owls. An agreement between the Wildlife Trust and Lincolnshire County Council – the first of its kind in the country when it was first set up in 1960 – entrusts the protection and management of some sixty of the county's specially important verges to the Trust which consults adjoining owners as necessary. Sixteen of these verges occur in the Wolds from Brocklesby in the north to Welton in the south.

Other Grasslands

In the Spilsby Sandstone country of the southern Wolds grasslands support a sparser flora characteristic of more acidic soils. One of the most attractive of their plants is the silvery-white meadow saxifrage which occurs in abundance in the Wildlife Trust's Silverines Meadow reserve at Goulceby, and occasionally elsewhere. Other reserves at Snipe Dales, Sow Dale and Furze Hill are also typical of the southern Wold valley grasslands. By their stream sides grow water forgetmenot, water mint, spotted orchid, ragged robin, fleabane and marsh thistle. Their bird populations too are rich and varied: kestrel and sparrowhawk, barn and tawny owls, snipe, green woodpecker, meadow pipit, sedge and grasshopper warblers and whitethroat. Badgers are particularly numerous in this countryside with setts in copses, open hillsides and roadside banks. The Trust's reserves, where traditional grazing by sheep and cattle has been maintained or restored, are now relics of a landscape and habitat which over large areas has been transformed in the last 50 years by ploughing and draining for more intensive arable cultivation. Agri-environment schemes, however, are already helping to restore grassland and wetland in areas of the poorest of these soils.

FIGURE 73. Pyramidal orchid.
GEOFF TRINDER

FIGURE 74. Skylark.
LINCOLNSHIRE WILDLIFE TRUST

Top:

FIGURE 75 *(left)*. Common blue butterfly.
BRIAN REDMAN

FIGURE 76 *(centre)*. Buzzards are back over the Wolds.
GEOFF TRINDER

FIGURE 77 *(right)*. Goldfinch.
GEOFF TRINDER

BELOW:

FIGURE 78 *(left)*. Harvest mouse.
GEOFF TRINDER

FIGURE 79 *(right)*. Rigsby Wood nature reserve on the eastern edge of the Wolds at bluebell time.
BARRIE WILKINSON

Rivers, Streams and Marshes

Most of the streams that drain the Wolds flow east to the sea like the Waithe Beck, the Lud, the Long Eau and Great Eau. In their upper reaches on the chalk they are clean, swift-flowing, stony-bedded streams with a characteristic diversity of invertebrates such as water beetles, caddisflies, stoneflies, mayflies and flatworms. Small fishes include brown trout, dace, chub, stone loach, brook lamprey and grayling which occurs in the Great Eau or Calceby Beck as it is known in its upper reaches. The Lymn – Tennyson's Brook – flows largely over the Lower Cretaceous strata of Spilsby Sandstone and Kimmeridge Clay; whilst the Bain, the longest of the Wold rivers, flows south through glacial sands and gravels in a broadening valley to join the Witham. The native crayfish used to occur in the Bain but, as in so many other British rivers, it has been displaced by the introduced larger American species. Kingfishers breed regularly on the Bain and occasionally on the other rivers, whilst otters have returned in recent years to both the Bain and the Lymn. Migrant and winter visitors to these streams include green sandpiper, grey wagtail and occasionally dipper.

Sand and gravel deposits in several of the Wold valleys have been exploited, notably on the Bain at Biscathorpe, Hemingby and Kirkby on Bain leaving wetland areas with increasingly varied bird populations. Two of the Kirkby lakes are nature reserves of the Wildlife Trust. In other places the rivers have been used to create fishing lakes.

Along the eastern edge of the Wolds at the base of the old cliff there is a spring line which gives rise to villages like Little Cawthorpe, Belleau, Well, Claxby and Welton. In several of these the springs form attractive pools with a specialized coldwater invertebrate fauna including a tiny flatworm *Crenobia alpina,* a rare species which may be an ice-age relict. The roadside spring and pool at Claxby is managed by the Wildlife Trust.

Many of the riverside pastures, meadows and marshes which supported nesting snipe and lapwing, and a varied flora including marsh orchids, were also drained and ploughed in the postwar period. Small marshy areas still survive in a few places, however, as in the Swaby and Calceby valleys and near Donington on Bain. Some restoration of river flood plains has been undertaken in recent years by the Environment Agency and the Drainage Boards – as on the Great Eau and Long Eau – and more such projects now seem likely.

In the years from 1940 to 1970 many of the lower reaches of the Wold streams were deepened and canalised in the interests of land drainage, as on the Lymn and the Waithe Beck. Since then however more enlightened treatment together with the consultation agreement between the responsible authorities, the Wildlife Trust and Natural England have preserved and in some cases restored the riverine features.

Woodland

There is little semi-natural woodland left in the chalk Wolds. The wood on Tetford Hill, an SSSI adjoining a Roadside Nature Reserve, is a rare example of the habitat. It is mainly ash with hazel and wych elm and some sycamore. Otherwise most of the Wold woodland consists of small plantations of sycamore, ash and conifers established after enclosure in the eighteenth and nineteenth centuries as amenity features and game coverts. A notable exception is the 3,000 acre expanse of mixed woodlands of beech, sycamore and conifers planted on the high ground of the northern Wolds on the Brocklesby estate between 1750 and 1950. These woods, managed from the outset according to the same policy, are of historic and landscape importance. Their bird interest is also considerable, but the ground flora is for the most part unremarkable.

Immediately below the former chalk cliff on the eastern edge of the Wolds, however, there are extensive semi-natural woodlands on the calcareous boulder clay of the Middle Marsh. These woods extend in a broken band from Legbourne in the north to Welton le Marsh in the south. Most of them are under 30 hectares in extent; only Burwell/Haugham (188 ha.) and the Welton High/Low/Willoughby Woods complex (169 ha.) are larger. They were managed for the most part as traditional coppice-with-standards, the standards of oak and ash, the coppice mainly of hazel and ash with abundant field maple, sallow, dogwood, guelder-rose and other shrubs. Alder and downy birch are also abundant in some of the wetter woods, and a few have patches of wych elm. Where inter-glacial sand occurs in the clays – as at Rigsby and Muckton – the flora is more diverse with species such as bluebell in abundance, primrose, wood

FIGURE 80. Bee orchid.
DAVID ROBINSON

anemone, woodruff, wood sorrel and occasional butterfly orchid and board-leaved helleborine. Herb Paris, a localized species, is also characteristic of these woods. On heavier clays ferns are abundant. Bird species are varied and two of the woods – Willoughby and Legbourne – contain heronries. The invertebrate fauna was somewhat impoverished in the 1960s by the loss of woodland fritillary butterflies, but the white admiral and speckled wood have recently recolonized some of the woods.

These woods are clearly only remnants of a once more extensive woodland cover in the area, as early place-names indicate. Much more was felled in the mid-nineteenth century years of Victorian high farming; and during the last 50 years about 380 of the 630 hectares (approximately 60%) of the ancient woodlands in this group have been replanted, mainly with conifers or conifer/broad-leaved mixtures. Coppicing had almost completely died out by the middle of the twentieth century, but in three of the woods, the Wildlife Trust reserves at Rigsby, Hoplands and Muckton (part), coppice has been renewed.

In the Spilsby Sandstone/Kimmeridge Clay valleys of the southern Wolds alder carrs form a distinctive and important group of woods. The higher slopes on the sandstone typically carry an abundance of bluebell and red campion; below the spring line on the wet floor of the valley dominated by alder and willow, marsh marigold and both species of golden saxifrage are characteristic of shady stream sides, while more open places have a tall herb community with yellow iris, giant horsetail, meadowsweet and angelica. Many of the smaller carrs have been eliminated by agricultural reclamation or degraded by tipping of agricultural refuse, but Keal Carr and the upper parts of both Sow Dale and Snipe Dales – all Wildlife Trust reserves – provide some of the best surviving examples.

Farmland

For nearly two hundred years arable farming has been the principal land use of the chalk Wolds. Large fields were created by enclosures and have remained so. Well managed hedges, road and track verges, hillside and roadside copses were otherwise the main wildlife habitats. Grassland was largely confined to valley bottoms and steep hillsides some of which were planted for amenity or game preservation purposes.

FIGURE 81. Snipe Dales nature reserve in the southern sandstone Wolds.
DAVID ROBINSON

There was some loss of hedgerows in the more intensive farming of the second half of the last century, but on the whole the landscape of the higher parts of the Wolds has changed less than that of some other areas – the adjoining Middle Marsh or Spilsby Sandstone country, for example. What has changed, however, as in most arable areas, has been the change in cropping and methods of cultivation. The old four-course rotation system designed to sustain soil fertility, was abandoned, and cropping became more intensive and continuous with the massive use of chemicals as fertilizers, herbicides and pesticides. All that together with the switch from spring to autumn sown grain has eliminated winter stubble with its abundance of weed seeds which support birds such as grey partridge and corn bunting, typical birds of chalk country which have declined drastically on the Wolds and elsewhere in recent years. Lapwing and skylark find autumn sown cereals too high for nesting by the spring. Both have declined, the lapwing especially being now a rarity as a breeding species although large flocks of immigrants occur in winter. Other animals affected by these agricultural changes are small mammals such as field vole and wood mouse, the scarcity of which reduces the numbers of barn owls and other predators. Another animal of arable landscapes which has undergone a slow decline is the brown hare.

More recent trends have helped to mitigate the damage to wildlife on farmland. Set-aside resulted in areas left uncultivated mainly for short periods; and now Environmental Stewardship and other schemes offer more positive incentives to environmentally sensitive farming methods. These schemes are encouraging the establishment of conservation headlands and uncultivated field margin strips which maintain invertebrate populations and cornfield 'weeds', and these in turn encourage seed-eating birds and predators. These developments are evident now in many parts of the Wolds and will help towards the restoration of biodiversity.

FIGURE 82. Lapwing.
DAVID ROBINSON
COLLECTION

CHAPTER TWELVE

Leisure and Tourism in the Wolds

Penny Baker

The steep-sided hills and picturesque rolling landscapes of the Wolds give a lie to the claim that Lincolnshire is flat and uninteresting. There are vantage points from which the views are enormous: to the silhouette of the towers of Lincoln Cathedral in one direction and across to the coast in another; to the cooling towers of power stations on the Trent and then over to the towers of the Humber Bridge and the landmark Grimsby Dock Tower. Visitors should pause at viewpoints on the ancient Bluestone Heath Road or on the crest of the Red Hill nature reserve near Goulceby and enjoy the intimate landscapes of hill and vale, and then will understand why the Wolds is an Area of Outstanding Natural Beauty. Stand in the porch of St Helen's church at West Keal and there in front of you is the expanse of the nearly flat fens punctuated on the horizon by the tall tower of St Botoloph's church, Boston, known, paradoxically, as The Stump. Nowhere else can one enjoy such vistas except from the Lincolnshire Wolds.

The northern Wolds are more open and gently rolling; the higher level-topped central Wolds are dissected by deep stunt-headed valleys, while the

FIGURE 83. Tourists looking over the southern Wolds by one of the information boards.
DERRICK FURLONG

FIGURE 84. Cycling in
the Wolds.
DERRICK FURLONG

southern sandstone Wolds with tree-lined secluded vales have a special intimate
character of their own. Villages and hamlets tend to be hidden away, their name
endings revealing their ancient past – Saxon hams and tons and Danish bys and
thorpes. And yet it has always been a farmed landscape, once of sheep walks
and rabbit warrens and now of intensive arable, tempered by modern schemes
of stewardship and diversification.

Not so long ago the Wolds was a place to be passed through on the way
to seaside resorts on the wet skirt of Lincolnshire. Now the Wolds have been
discovered by new visitors as landscapes to be explored and enjoyed in their own
right, on a bicycle and on foot – the long distance Viking Way traverses the length
of the Wolds – as well as by car. Poet Laureate Alfred, Lord Tennyson, born in
the Wolds at Somersby, wrote of haunts of ancient peace, and there are still places
which have that feel, tucked away and in contrast to the open tops.

Consider a few statistics: 97 scheduled monuments including classic deserted
medieval villages, 15 Sites of Special Scientific Interest including nature reserves
managed by the Lincolnshire Wildlife Trust, and 282 sites of nature conservation
importance including Regionally Important Geological Sites and Protected
Roadside Verges. The stunning tree-lined gorge of Hubbard's Hills has been
prized by the people of Louth since it became England's second country park
in 1907. Before that it had been a destination for day trips by train from
Lincoln during Factory Week; today it is being rediscovered by tourists on a
day out from the coast. At the Snipe Dales Country Park and Nature Reserve
waymarked paths enable visitors on foot and in wheelchairs to explore its woods
and valleys, and seek out the line of the Greenwich Meridian from which the
world's time is measured.

Snipe Dales is managed for the County Council by the Lincolnshire Wildlife
Trust and is an example of how it is possible to balance the pressures of tourism

FIGURE 85. Action on the
2¼ mile Cadwell Park
circuit in 1980.
RICHARD WEBB

and quiet recreation with the need to conserve the very features of landscape and wildlife that people come to enjoy. Local people have long enjoyed a walk in Snipe Dales, but now it is increasingly a destination for visitors from further afield.

Taking the Wolds as a whole, there are about a million day visitors a year, and some 60,000 stay overnight. UK visitors stay for three or four days, but those from overseas stay longer. The Wolds and the AONB in particular are increasingly recognised as a desirable tourist destination, and it is not unusual to hear comments such as 'I had no idea there was so much variety to explore and enjoy. Why haven't I heard of it before? I must come back again.' With increasing visitor numbers comes the challenge of balancing the rural economy with the demands of tourists looking for new destinations and new experiences. The Wolds have become one of the latter, but with it comes the need to ensure they retain their natural charm.

That is where the role of market towns fringing the Wolds comes in, since it is there that most of the accommodation is to be found. Louth is one of the best of Lincolnshire market towns and regarded as the cultural capital of east Lincolnshire. Its greatest man-made treasures are the perfect Perpendicular steeple of St James's church, the tallest parish church spire in England, and the mid-nineteenth century panorama of the town, painted from the top of the spire, and reckoned to be among the best in Europe. Add to them a repertory theatre, the leading independent museum in the county, a multi-screen cinema, a range of cultural and sporting activities, unspoilt medieval streets and Georgian buildings, family-run shops, thrice weekly street markets, a beast market, hotels, tea rooms, pubs and self-catering accommodation, and here is an ideal base for exploring the Wolds. Louth is also renowned for its food and named as one of the best market towns in Britain by TV chef Rick Stein.

FIGURE 86. Ramblers' window in All Saints, Walesby (The Ramblers' Church) high on the western edge of the Wolds.
LINCOLNSHIRE WOLDS COUNTRYSIDE SERVICE

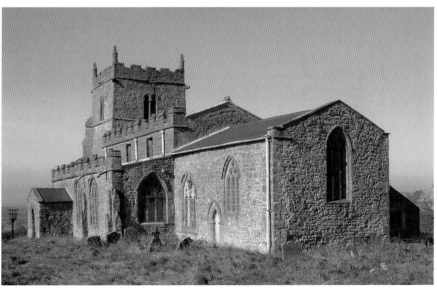

Also on the eastern fringe is Alford, with a five-sail working windmill, a restored seventeenth-century manor house and summer craft markets. Alford was the birthplace of preacher and first American feminist Anne Hutchinson who founded the State of Rhode Island, and from whom Presidents Roosevelt

FIGURE 87. The South
Wold Hunt meet at the
Blue Bell Inn, Belchford.
DERRICK FURLONG

FIGURE 88. Walkers on a
public right of way in the
Wolds.
LINCOLNSHIRE WOLDS
COUNTRYSIDE SERVICE

and Bush are said to be descended. On the southern edge are Spilsby, birthplace
of Sir John Franklin the Arctic explorer, and Horncastle, the antiques centre
of Lincolnshire, its many inns recalling the town's past status of hosting the
largest horse fair in the world, and with links to Sir Joseph Banks of Revesby,
the 'Father of Australia'. Captain John Smith, founder of Virginia and eventually

FIGURE 89 *(left)*. A
refurbished traditional
signpost in the northern
Wolds.
LINCOLNSHIRE WOLDS
COUNTRYSIDE SERVICE

FIGURE 90 *(right)*. Horse
riders pause by the ford
at Biscathorpe.
DERRICK FURLONG

the USA, was born in the Marsh village of Willoughby and went to school in
Alford and Louth.

On the western edge of the Wolds are Market Rasen with its attractive
steeplechase course, and the Roman settlement of Caistor. All with a range
of inns and locally produced Taste of Lincolnshire foods, each as a gateway
to the Wolds, a starting point for a tour and leisurely walks or a serious trek.
The annual Wolds Walking Festival in May offers the opportunity to enjoy the
choice of some fifty guided walks to suit all ages and abilities. There is also
an equestrian centre at Kenwick near Louth and opportunities elsewhere for
exploring the countryside on horseback.

Cadwell Park, hidden in the hills south of Louth, is one of the county's
secrets, except to the motor-racing fraternity. Created in 1934 as a rough race-
track for motorcycles, with a fearsome 'mountain' feature, it has become a mecca
for cars and karts as well. The present 2.25 miles tarmac layout, built in 1962
with dips and crests, is a distinctive and exciting venue with natural slopes for
spectator viewing. The highlight of the racing calendar is the British Superbikes
Championship which draws extra-large crowds.

Some twenty percent of Britain's food comes from Lincolnshire, which has
its own specialities – Lincoln Red beef, Poacher cheese, Lincolnshire sausages,
game birds and plumbread, washed down with locally brewed beer – all from in
or near the Wolds and obtainable in the market towns and served in village inns
and cafes. 'Taste of Lincolnshire' foods, the attraction of the natural landscape
and traditional market towns combine to make tourism one of the key drivers
of the Wolds economy.

Good Friday on Red Hill

Every Good Friday morning since 1965 (except 2001 when foot and mouth disease restrictions were in force) the Red Hill nature reserve on the steep Wolds edge overlooking Goulceby is the scene of a unique event in Lincolnshire to mark the anniversary of the crucifixion of Christ. Three wooden crosses are carried in silent procession from the bottom of the hill, pausing three times for a gospel reading and quiet reflection. The crosses are then erected on the top of the hill while below in the grassy hollow of the former chalk quarry the priest in charge of the Asterby Group Parish leads a service of prayers, readings and hymns, accompanied by the Horncastle Silver Band. Whatever the weather, scores of people congregate from far and wide, leaving the crosses stark against the sky where they will stay until after celebrations of Christ's resurrection on Easter Sunday. And from the top of Red Hill on a clear day one can see the three towers of Lincoln Cathedral silhouetted against the western skyline.

David Robinson

Good Friday service on the nature reserve at Red Hill.
DAVID ROBINSON COLLECTION

CHAPTER THIRTEEN

Birth of the AONB

Ray Taylor

The first recorded reference to a national landscape designation for the Wolds occurred during a debate of the Executive Committee of the Lincolnshire Branch of the Council for the Protection of Rural England (CPRE) on 8 March 1966. Mrs Phy Ais West had expressed the hope that the newly established Countryside Committee of Lindsey County Council could be persuaded to turn the Wolds into a National Park, and Ted Smith welcomed this as a 'splendid idea'. At the next meeting on 17 May 1966, Richard Pepler, Deputy Clerk to the county and a keen member of the CPRE, explained that a national park must have regard to the facilities offered for open air recreation. In view of the nature of the Wolds, he felt the area would not be suitable for a national park but could be designated as an 'Area of Outstanding Natural Beauty'. The minutes of the previous meeting were altered accordingly!

A letter was then sent to the Clerk of the County Council, and on 15 June the County Planning Officer, Robert Stirling, wrote informally to Reg Hookway, Chief Technical Officer of the National Parks Commission, inviting him to visit the Wolds. The first substantive meeting between officers of the County Council and the Commission took place on 7 November 1966, when it was acknowledged that although the charm of the Wolds 'derives from the undulating terrain, sparse settlement pattern and excellent views, it seemed obvious to all present that, in the national context, the Wolds did not rate sufficiently highly to warrant AONB designation'. The notes of the meeting made by Commission officers went on to explain that 'the Lindsey officers were happy to receive this negative response. They will advise their committee accordingly'.

This they duly did, passing the news to the CPRE Branch in a letter from Walter Lane, Clerk to the County Council, dated 4 January 1967, in which he revealed that 'in all the circumstances the Planning and Countryside Committees have concluded that no useful purpose would be served at present by making a formal request to the Commission'. The Commission were then informed on 10 January 1967 of the Committee's decision and that was presumed to be that.

However, despite no further correspondence and with no evidence of any developments on the files of either the Commission or the County Council, the Lincolnshire Wolds resurfaced once more nine months later. On 31 October 1967, the National Park Commissioners considered a paper which outlined a proposed future programme of AONB designations. It set out 'the official list of candidates for possible designation', comprising thirteen areas that had been suggested in Arthur Hobhouse's report of 1947 and a further fifteen – including the Lincolnshire Wolds – that had not.

An officer of the Commission was forthwith despatched to carry out a site inspection of this newly – and suddenly – proposed AONB. Whether this officer had suffered a particularly bad Christmas, or whether he experienced particularly inclement conditions, is not recorded. However, from his visit on 27 December 1967 he produced a particularly jaundiced report in which he advised the Commission to reconsider their decision to designate the Wolds as an AONB. 'If, in spite of everything,' he wrote, 'they should decide to go ahead, I can only say that it is likely to be a very sub-standard affair; far better country than this has been excluded from AONBs elsewhere as not being up to standard. In my opinion, these Wolds simply do not possess the necessary landscape ingredients from which AONBs are made.' And in a phrase most hurtful to all Lincolnshire Yellowbellies, he concluded that 'although Tennyson – a native – wrote poetry about it, it is quite understandable that he should have preferred to live in the Isle of Wight'.

Notwithstanding these views, on 5 February the County Council were informed that the Commission would be willing to consider designation and expressed the hope that 'with the help of the (County) Council this designation may prove to be expeditious and productive of good results in the preservation and enhancement of the beautiful areas concerned'.

Discussions over the boundary of the proposed area were pursued and on 24 October 1968 the same officer of the newly named Countryside Commission who had previously expressed such grave reservations over the landscape quality of the Wolds met the County Planning Officer before being taken on a tour of the area. The change of season had done nothing to mellow his views and he reported that 'one travels through mile after mile of comparatively dull, quite ordinary farming country of no particular scenic attraction; much of it no better country than can be seen almost anywhere throughout rural Britain......Mr Stirling is delighted by the Commission's decision to proceed towards designation, and I think this has probably had the effect of giving (the County Council) a rather exaggerated idea about the scenic merits of the Lincolnshire Wolds'. He then reminded his superiors that his previous report and landscape appraisal had been withheld from the Commission and that this was the first time it had taken a decision to designate an area 'blind'. He therefore recommended that some members of the Commission should visit the area in order to satisfy themselves that the landscape quality of the Wolds justified AONB designation.

This officer appears to have had his way, for on 1 May 1969 the Commission wrote to the County Council indicating that 'circumstances have recently arisen which have made it impossible for us to take the question of an area of outstanding natural beauty in Lincolnshire any further for the time being'. Without further explanation the letter went on to state that the Commission

FIGURE 91. The Scamblesby Vale from Cawkwell Hill about the time of the AONB designation.
HUGH MARTINEAU

could not be recommended to accept a large part of the proposed area because 'the area was far from homogeneous' (although homogeneity had never been revealed as a ground for designation), and 'a very large part of it was found to be below the standard required for designation by virtue of the number of disfigurements, notably many large overhead electricity lines, television masts and indifferent landscape which had been stripped of its trees and hedges'.

Despite this setback, a further paper was presented to the Commission on 3 June 1969 explaining why it was urgent that someone (ie. commissioners) should visit the area. The minutes of that meeting record 'a minor disagreement with Professor McGregor who formally declared that he *liked* prairie landscapes so what was wrong with them!' The Chairman of the Commission, it seems, was also sceptical about AONBs in general, and other members requested a further paper for a future meeting.

As a result the Commissioners agreed 'that it would be desirable for members to visit the area and study its landscape characteristics but they considered it would be inappropriate to proceed further with designation until they had reviewed their general policy in this respect'. This decision was conveyed to the County Council on 18 June and, not surprisingly, brought forth considerable dismay, encapsulated in a letter of 22 August from Walter Lane, Clerk to the Council, to Mervyn Bell, Secretary of the Commission: 'Your letter was received here with dismay....

Information that probably Lindsey is the only County Council whose proposals are being deferred in this way only serves to increase our disappointment…. To be told simply that the matter is to be deferred for an unspecified period is both discouraging and frustrating…. I would urge most strongly that the decision to defer the Lincolnshire Wolds proposal be reconsidered.'

It was therefore agreed at the Commission's meeting on 7 October to explain to the Clerk that 'they had not decided to turn down the proposal….but to defer consideration while giving thought to AONB designation policy'. They also hoped that the Deputy Chairman, James Fisher, and (in what was probably the most fortuitous decision of the whole saga) Professor McGregor (who 'liked prairie landscapes') 'would be able to visit Lincolnshire shortly'. This they did and at the Commission's meeting on 4 November 1969 the pendulum swung once more when 'both Mr Fisher and Professor McGregor strongly supported the County Council's desire for the area to be designated as an AONB'.

The County Council were then asked to redefine the proposed area when, in a letter dated 18 November, the Commission explained their preference for 'the boundaries to follow some clear, recognisable and reasonably permanent feature on the ground. For example, roads, watercourses, railway lines and ownership boundaries would be better than undefined footpaths, or field boundaries such as fences, hedgerows or walls'. Why an ownership boundary was considered more recognisable and reasonably permanent on the ground than a hedgerow or wall was not explained. Perhaps it implied something of the timelessness of landownership in Lincolnshire in contrast to the volatility of modern agricultural techniques.

Meanwhile, Lindsey County Council were carrying out an initial consultation by circulating copies of a plan showing the proposed boundaries of the AONB to Rural District Councils, to the Lincolnshire Trust for Nature Conservation and the CPRE. The general reaction of the District Councils was, to say the least, reserved. There was a general feeling that there had been insufficient time for consultation and, in any case, most of the local councils were, in the words of Horncastle RDC, 'well aware of the natural beauty of the Wolds and took this into account in implementing their policies'.

Horncastle RDC 'questioned whether there was any necessity to prescribe the area as they have no information of undesirable development, either existing or proposed, which constitutes a threat to the area and could not be dealt with under ordinary planning procedure. The proposal is at the moment viewed by the Council with a certain amount of apprehension'. This official view was expressed more rhetorically in the personal contribution to the debate by Councillor Hallowes, when he asked 'Do we want to be hamstrung from above? Are we not the best persons to preserve our heritage of the Wolds? Do we want to advertise that it exists? Isn't it better to leave the area as it is and it will only attract those visitors who appreciate the countryside and its ancient buildings and churches?' Spilsby RDC required two meetings to reach their decision in favour of the AONB proposal, despite the strong views of Councillor Charles Read who had called the

FIGURE 92. Walter Lane (later CBE), Clerk to Lindsey County Council 1957–1974.
LINDSEY COUNTY COUNCIL

proposals 'dictatorial', and the CPRE 'a group of interfering busybodies'.

The Lincolnshire Trust, not surprisingly for one of those bodies with allegedly 'extreme views on conservation', supported the proposal. Their submission was principally devoted to urging an extension of the designated area to include the wooded south-eastern corner of the Wolds, and suggesting, in less forceful terms, the inclusion of the Spilsby sandstone area as far south as Old Bolingbroke and Keal, and the Brocklesby Estate with its adjacent 'tops' and scarp in the northern Wolds. At a special meeting of the CPRE on 20 March 1970, the Branch made a number of supportive suggestions, urging further consideration of extending the northern boundary towards Grimsby. At the southern end of the Wolds the CPRE went even further than the Lincolnshire Trust by proposing a greater extension to include Fulletby, Greetham, Winceby and Asgarby and Old Bolingbroke parishes.

The farming community had meanwhile been expressing concern about the designation, and this was formalised on 22 April 1970 when the Lincolnshire Executive of the National Farmers Union resolved that 'as representatives of the farming opinion, the Committee strongly opposed the introduction of such an order'. Members agreed that 'the Wolds were beautiful due to their being well farmed and not to natural beauty'.

By now the debate was firmly in the public arena. An (anonymous) Wolds resident, writing to the *Grimsby Evening Telegraph*, criticised 'the clumsy and unsympathetic' form and siting of some farm buildings, claiming that 'if the designation will impose higher standards of taste and design on the Wolds…. then everybody, including farmers, should be delighted'.

Nevertheless, hopes – and fears – remained high and the countryside columnist of the *Grimsby Evening Telegraph* attempted to bring reason to the debate with a well-balanced feature on 29 April 1970 in which he tried to see both sides of the argument. 'Many farmers', he wrote, 'take the view that the Wolds – as such – derive their beauty *because* they are well farmed; because the very pattern of husbandry shows to the best pictorial advantage the colours of soil, chalk, tree, wall and skyline; because the wonderful undulations with outcrops of stone under thin soils fascinate the artist; because the depopulation of the agricultural industry has meant that fewer new houses have been built. It is strongly argued that the Wolds without farming would be a very unremarkable stretch of sparsely-wooded low-elevation Eastern England… I believe that the farmer is still looking after the land, but for more realistic reasons. In order to survive he *has* to look after it, for it is the raw material of our great farming tradition… There is a great deal of jealousy, of misunderstanding, of historic nonsense talked about it. I suggest it is time for both sides to get together and talk some common sense.'

When the Commission eventually debated the principle of an AONB for the Wolds on 5 May 1970, they seemed a bit aggrieved that the County Council had already carried out some consultations before the Commission had approved a preliminary boundary and statement of intentions. James Fisher, the Vice-Chairman and one of the two Commissioners who had visited the Wolds, could not, however, contain his enthusiasm when he was reported as stating that 'he is in favour of the Commission approving the boundaries which the local planning authorities want, although we do not yet know precisely what these are'. The officers of the Commission recognised what now appeared to be a headlong gallop towards designation and, not wishing to be trampled in the rush, shrewdly recommended that 'notwithstanding the fact that a Statement of Intention is not yet available and that the boundary proposals are still somewhat confused, the Commission may agree that in all the circumstances the Lindsey County Council should be asked to proceed now to the full preliminary consultation stage'.

The NFU and Country Landowners Association eventually responded to the County Council's consultation on 9 and 26 October respectively. The NFU were 'strongly opposed' to the designation on the grounds that it 'may hinder natural development to the detriment of agricultural production and efficiency'. The CLA were rather more circumspect in their objection. Private correspondence following their committee's deliberations revealed that 'the objection to the proposed designation should give no reasons for objecting, beyond the fact that the case for designation appeared inadequate'.

An internal memorandum within the Countryside Commission at around this time noted, rather worryingly, that 'this designation is not proceeding in accordance with our normal requirements as to procedure. The Commission have not formally approved a preliminary map or boundary, or a draft Statement of Intention; and the Commission have not formally authorized or invited the Local Planning Authority to put in hand consultations.'

Nevertheless, in February 1971 when the recommendation to make a formal submission for the designation of the Wolds as an AONB was debated by the County Council, the *Grimsby Evening Telegraph* reported that landowning and farming interests made a determined attempt to reject the proposal. Sir John Maitland, a land-owning councillor from Harrington in the Wolds, contended that the Wolds had become an area of natural beauty from a far higher power than the Lindsey County Council'. Councillor Clow agreed, adding that 'they were granted to us from God and have always been with us'. Councillor Slaney, an 'urban' councillor from Cleethorpes, disagreed –'he had never heard such a lot of poppycock in his life…these country lads get up and are indignant when someone wants to attempt to do something'. The recommendation, he reminded members, was intended to strengthen the hand of farmers who had done a tremendous amount to preserve the Wolds. The frustration of the Planning Committee chairman, Alderman Cox, can be sensed when he expressed 'disappointment and surprise at the opposition to the proposal. No-one would deny the Wolds were an area of outstanding natural beauty, and the Planning Committee wanted to preserve and protect them as such in the interests of the farming community.' With this rallying cry no doubt still ringing in their ears, councillors defeated the reference back to committee 'by a large majority', and the recommendation was approved.

Following the County Council's formal resolution, a number of public meetings were arranged in the area. Whilst most views expressed were predictable, the meeting held in Louth and reported in the *Louth Standard*, revealed that 'when the chairman called for the views of a Wolds farmer… there were none present at the forum. "They are not very worried", was an audience comment.' The local NFU branch secretary, however, reiterating the well-rehearsed view that the 'beauty of the Wolds was in fact that they were so well farmed', added a new visual delight to the landscape in claiming 'it is a very exciting sight. When the crops grow it comes alive; that is the beauty of the Wolds.'

Nevertheless, the Countryside Commission went ahead and early in September 1972 designated the Wolds as an Area of Outstanding Natural Beauty. This was reported to the County Planning Committee on 5 October and 'noted with satisfaction' – not surprisingly after so many years of effort by the Committee and its predecessors.

The precise process that took place within the hallowed walls of the

Department of the Environment over the next few months go unrecorded. However, on 17 April 1973 the Secretary of State for the Environment duly confirmed the Commission's Order which belies its significance with its brevity. In its ninety-six words are enshrined the efforts, hopes and fears of many people with a genuine, albeit differing, perception of the Wolds and their value, their importance and their contribution to the life and landscape of Lincolnshire.

CHAPTER FOURTEEN

Managing the AONB

Steve Jack

The designation in 1973 of a large part of the Lincolnshire Wolds as an Area of Outstanding Natural Beauty confirmed the national importance of the Wolds and placed a primary duty on relevant local authorities to protect and enhance its 'natural beauty'. It also included the need to have particular regard to local communities and rural industries, and where possible to meet the demands for recreation. There have been many debates about what is meant by 'natural beauty', especially considering the major influence of farming on the Wolds landscape. However it is generally accepted to mean those special features that contribute to the high scenic quality and special character of the Wolds, including geology, topography, wildlife and historical features.

The Lincolnshire Wolds is today one of a family of forty-nine AONBs

FIGURE 93. A beech clump in winter.
DERRICK FURLONG

FIGURE 94. Improving
chalk streams is a project
in the Management Plan.
LINCOLNSHIRE WOLDS
COUNTRYSIDE SERVICE

in England, Wales and Northern Ireland, and quite different from the other chalkland landscapes of the Chilterns, North Wessex Downs and West Wiltshire Downs. Strong characteristics of the Wolds include its remoteness and tranquillity. Even on a Bank Holiday one can journey into the quieter areas, enjoy a walk and scarcely see another soul. This is both an asset and a threat, as there is a need to promote the area to visitors to help support the local economy, while ensuring that the peace and solitude of the Wolds are not harmed.

The AONB designation was followed by local government reorganisation a year later creating East and West Lindsey District Councils and Cleethorpes District Council (later part of North East Lincolnshire Council) each with boundaries including part of the AONB. Forward planning and development control issues were thus spread across different authorities and provided a high level of protection – in planning terms equivalent in many respects to the country's National Parks.

There was, however, a growing concern that management arrangements for AONBs were unclear and far from ideal, whilst National Parks were provided

FIGURE 95. Multi-colours
of an evolving landscape.
DERRICK FURLONG

with funding support from central government and commonly operated as
a single planning and administrative authority. Since the Wolds designation,
pressures on the landscape have increased, especially trends in farming to
improve productivity through increased mechanisation. Government grants
through the 1960s and 1970s provided incentives to drain wet ground, remove
hedgerows and develop economies of scale in pursuit of ever higher yields,
and the Wolds was no different from other areas of the country in seeing the
effects.

By the late 1980s there was growing recognition and concern about the
continuing changes in the Wolds landscape, many of which were beyond
the remit of the planning control system. In response, the local authorities
supported by the then Countryside Commission, established the Lincolnshire
Wolds Countryside Management Project in 1991. Its initial focus was to
encourage landscape restoration schemes, with an additional remit of improving
the opportunities for countryside recreation. Two project officers were
employed to work in East and West Lindsey respectively, and they quickly
set about supporting landowners and communities in positive countryside
management.

Following the establishment of the Project team there was growing
acceptance of the need for a wider management partnership to improve
information and advice to the core partnership of local authorities and the
Countryside Commission. It could also bring additional benefits of improving
wider dissemination of the importance and value of the AONB designation.

A milestone was the establishment of a Wolds Forum, a wide group of people from public, private and voluntary sector agencies, many of whom had an active and specialist interest in the Wolds.

The importance of the Lincolnshire Wolds AONB in a national context was further acknowledged and recognised with the publication of the Lincolnshire Wolds Landscape Assessment in 1993. It was undertaken by Cobham Resource Consultants with assistance and advice from local specialists on the Wolds Forum, and was sponsored by the Countryside Commission. It was very much a benchmark study, highlighting the special qualities of the Wolds and identifying four landscape character areas: the north-west scarp, the chalk wolds, the ridges and valleys of the south-west, and the south-eastern claylands. The report confirmed that the Lincolnshire Wolds continued to meet the national criteria for AONB designation stating, 'the area has a combination of features that is unusual, or even unique in a national context. Visually it is a delight to visit, and its aesthetic qualities are matched by a special concentration of geological and heritage features of national importance. The area has significant cultural associations, notably the link with Tennyson, and is highly valued by local residents and visitors'. The special qualities contributing to the Wolds outstanding landscape were listed as the unique physiography, the scenic, working landscape, the impressive archaeological interest, and the area's valued cultural landscape. The report was influential in raising awareness of the AONB, and helped to encourage, guide and influence those responsible for policies and management.

In 1995 the local partnership acknowledged the obligation to safeguard the AONB landscapes and building on the early successes of the Wolds Countryside Project, the Forum endorsed the decision to merge the two project areas, establishing the Lincolnshire Wolds Countryside Service. This represented an important shift in the management of the AONB, creating a single dedicated staff unit. Management arrangements were formalised in 1998 with the establishment of a Joint Advisory Committee, commonly referred to as the JAC.

Many of the representatives on the former Wolds Forum continued to serve on the JAC which, under Councillor Mrs Sheila Roy as its first Chairman, ensured that administration and guidance were in place in accordance with national government recommendations. As well as instructing the Lincolnshire Wolds Countryside Service, whose first manager was Paul Holley, the JAC instigated production of one of the earliest Management Plan documents for any AONB in the country. This comprehensive document was completed in 1998 and recognised the importance of the Lincolnshire Wolds as a living and working landscape, requiring the effective balancing of environmental, social and economic principles. In many ways the document was ahead of its time, although it lacked the necessary statutory clout and resources to initiate a truly partnership-wide action plan for the Wolds.

The production of the Lincolnshire Wolds AONB Management Plan was

FIGURE 96. Rolling
Wolds near Tetford.
DERRICK FURLONG

particularly timely as nationally there was growing anxiety over the increased
development pressures on all the AONBs in England and Wales. Unlike the
National Parks, during the 1990s there were still limited statutory powers and
dedicated national funds to assist local authorities with their protection and
management. The National Association for AONBs, together with professional
and academic advocates, had long campaigned for strengthened legislation and
increased government support for AONBs. Similarly, a number of government
consultations and policy statements throughout the 1990s had recommended
improvements.

Years of national campaigning finally bore fruit with the passing of the
Countryside and Rights of Way (CRoW) Act in 2000. Sections 89 and 90
created important new powers for AONBs. Crucially the statute placed a
requirement on all relevant local authorities to produce, adopt and publish
an AONB Management Plan that would require review every five years. The
legislation was backed by an improved funding stream through the Countryside
Agency with an initial three year funding package of £17 million spread across
all the AONBs. The news was officially announced by the then Environment
Minister, Michael Meacher proclaiming that *our AONBs are the cinderellas of
our landscape heritage.* It was hoped the new arrangements would rebalance the

FIGURE 97. Winter on
the Wolds.
DAVID ROBINSON

apparent disparity of resources between National Parks and AONBs. As Mike Taylor, Chief Executive Officer of the National Association of AONBs, would provocatively report at their annual National Conference in 2008, AONBs were still excellent value to the taxpayer, costing under 15p per person per annum compared with 70p for the National Parks!

Throughout the 1990s the small and committed Lincolnshire Wolds Countryside Service established excellent links with the local farming community, chiefly through providing advice and financial support in the form of modest grant schemes. The grants programme proved especially popular with landowners, often assisting them with tree planting, hedge planting and laying, creation of small copses, and restoration of other landscape features such as beech clumps, traditional meadows and ponds. The Countryside Service also provided a much needed way of increasing local awareness of the special features of the Wolds, establishing a popular programme of guided walks and events.

The introduction of the CRoW Act provided a change in direction for the Countryside Service as there was an increasing challenge to think and operate strategically whilst also maintaining and enhancing strong ties with local communities. The Act also helped to strengthen and formalise local partnership funding arrangements for the AONB. A governance review decided to expand the Countryside Service to a core staff of four. Although small in comparison to larger AONBs, it was considered sufficient until the development of additional projects.

Around the same time Lincolnshire County Council commissioned an innovative exercise to test and develop an Interpretation Strategy for the

Wolds. Its starting point was a general concern over the socio-economic issues facing the rural communities in and around the Wolds, not least the continuing perceived reliance on agriculture and its support services. The Interpretation Strategy helped to highlight the opportunities for promoting the Wolds through increased recreation and tourism initiatives, which could help encourage farm diversification as well as supporting important rural services such as village shops, tea rooms and pubs. The consultation highlighted the need for a cautious, well planned approach which would ensure that any future tourism/recreation developments were seen as appropriate to the area both in scale and in landscape design. The Strategy was officially endorsed by the JAC in October 2001 and provided the partnership with a renewed mandate for exploring collaborative projects that could help to inform both residents and visitors of the special qualities of the Wolds.

The work involved in developing the Interpretation Strategy was an important precursor and aid to developing the first statutory Management Plan for the AONB, it being a statutory obligation for local authorities to produce such a plan. The Countryside Service, guided by the JAC, co-ordinated the review of the original 1998 Plan, initially by community consultations across the Wolds under the banner – 'Celebrating the Past, Planning for the Future'. This helped to inform both the revised Management Strategy and its accompanying Action Plan. Over 460 public responses were received from a questionnaire and the responses helped to identify issues people felt were important to the area. The findings reinforced the value placed on the scenery and sweeping

FIGURE 98. An Open Day at the former gravel quarry at Welton le Wold: visitors learning about the geological importance of the site in understanding phases of the last Ice Age.
DAVID ROBINSON

views in the Wolds and its peace and tranquillity. There was, however, public concern over increasing threats to the loss of scenic beauty through changes to landscape features and the impact of unsightly development including large agriculture buildings, pylons and telecommunication masts. The consultations highlighted a degree of polarisation of views between those wishing to develop a strategy of promotion and small scale development to help safeguard services and communities, and a smaller but vocal group who wished to see very little development or promotion of the area for fear of harm to the character and charm of the Wolds.

The community consultation and subsequent peer and public reviews helped to guide the Countryside Service and the JAC in producing the Lincolnshire Wolds AONB Management Plan 2004–09, published in April 2004 and adopted by Lincolnshire County Council, East Lindsey District Council, West Lindsey District Council and North East Lincolnshire Council. The document is comprehensive, summarising the special features and qualities of the AONB, identifying current issues facing the area including threats and pressures, and setting out policy, objectives and action for protecting and sustaining the AONB – its landscape, wildlife, heritage, cultural value and the people who live and work there. The Plan helped to formulate a shared vision:

> The Lincolnshire Wolds will continue to be a vibrant living and working landscape through the primary influence of sustainable agriculture, forestry and land management. It will retain its unique and nationally important sense of place: an area of open rolling hills, dramatic views, farmed fields changing with the seasons, tranquil valleys, woodland pasture, streams and attractive villages.
>
> The Wolds natural and cultural heritage will be well known, enjoyed and widely respected by both residents and visitors. It will continue to provide a place of tranquillity and inspiration for those fortunate enough to visit the area, whilst meeting the economic, social and environmental needs of those who live and work there.

This vision acknowledges the challenges of securing social, economic and environmental progress that will conserve and enhance the special and intrinsic qualities that define the Lincolnshire Wolds AONB.

Following the launch of the Plan, the JAC and the Countryside Service have worked closely with local residents, landowners and like-minded organisations to take forward initiatives and projects. One of the most influential has been the development of the Lincolnshire Wolds Sustainable Development Fund. Following a successful application to the East Midlands Development Agency, the Lincolnshire Wolds was the first English AONB to create such a fund. The initial pilot scheme had a £75,000 delegated fund for local community and business projects that helped to protect and enhance the AONB whilst also securing socio-economic benefits. The pilot proved immensely popular, with over 150 enquiries from which eleven applications were funded. Its success contributed to the national roll out of a Sustainable Development Fund to all AONBs, with support from Defra and the Countryside Agency. Following the

FIGURE 99. Heritage of the Wolds map from the *Wonders of the Wolds* leaflet series.

LINCOLNSHIRE AND SOUTH HUMBERSIDE TOURISM AND LINCOLNSHIRE WOLDS COUNTRYSIDE SERVICE

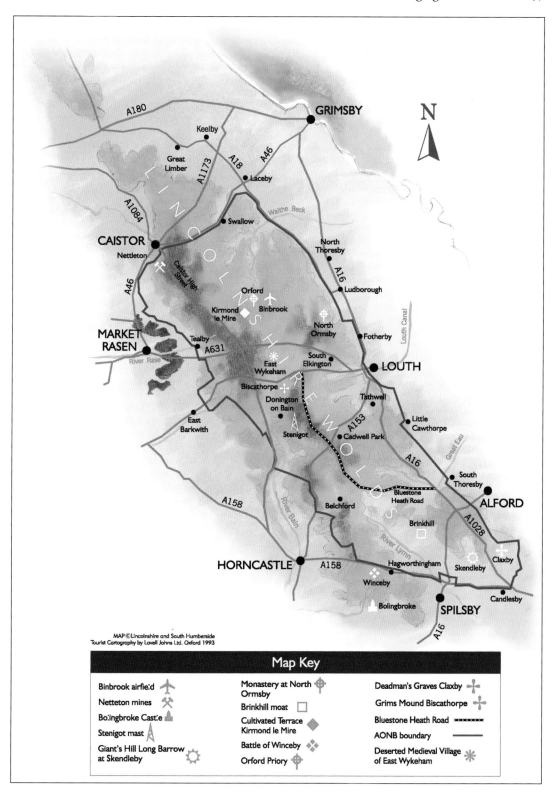

MAP © Lincolnshire and South Humberside
Tourist Cartography by Lovell Johns Ltd. Oxford 1993

Map Key

Binbrook airfield ✈	Monastery at North Ormsby ✠	Deadman's Graves Claxby ✞
Netteton mines ⚒	Brinkhill moat ☐	Grims Mound Biscathorpe ✞
Bolingbroke Castle ▲	Cultivated Terrace Kirmond le Mire ◆	Bluestone Heath Road ▬▬▬
Stenigot mast ⋀	Battle of Winceby ❖	AONB boundary ———
Giant's Hill Long Barrow at Skendleby ✺	Orford Priory ✠	Deserted Medieval Village of East Wykeham ✲

pilot, the Countryside Service successfully delegated £225,000 of funding from the Countryside Agency and the County Sub-Regional Strategic Partnership Lincolnshire Enterprise in 2005/06 and 2006/07 to support a further 32 local projects. These ranged from the renovation of community buildings to a school outreach programme in partnership with the Freiston Study Centre. The Countryside Service continues to oversee a Wolds Sustainable Development Fund, providing opportunities for local action in harmony with the Management Plan.

Other recent success stories for the Countryside Service and the JAC include the restoration of traditional roadsigns in the Wolds, with over a hundred refurbished, setting up the Chalk Streams Partnership to restore and promote the importance of such streams in the Wolds, the further development of a hugely popular series of walk and information leaflets and programmes of events, and establishment of the annual Lincolnshire Wolds Walking Festival.

Despite very uncertain financial times for future public spending it is reassuring that Natural England – the new government agency and successor to the Countryside Agency, English Nature and the Rural Development Service, has recognised the importance of all AONB landscapes at the national level, pledging in 2008 a further three years of central government funding to support local authority funding arrangements. This announcement coincides with the 60th anniversary of the original 1949 National Park and Access to the Countryside Act which provided the original legislative framework for establishing AONBs. In 2009 the Lincolnshire Wolds AONB is being recognised in local, regional and national circles via the "Diamonds in the Landscape" – a joint campaign of celebration undertaken by all AONBs and National Parks to highlight the richness and diversity of these nationally important places.

There is still much work to be done, and the success of managing the Wolds will ultimately depend on continuing to achieve real actions and positive outcomes on the ground. Change is inevitable, bearing in mind the living and working nature of the landscape and the growing uncertainties of climate change. However, partnerships of local farmers, communities, the wider public and organisations represented on the Wolds Joint Advisory Committee will be crucial to balance environmental, social and economic progress with our duty to safeguard the unique charm and character of the Lincolnshire Wolds for generations to come.

Further Reading

Chapter 1

H. H. Swinnerton and P. E. Kent (1981) *The Geology of Lincolnshire.* Lincoln

A. Straw (2007) *The Last Two Glaciations of Lincolnshire.* Louth

A. Straw (2006) *Glacial and Pre-Glacial Deposits at Welton le Wold, Lincolnshire.* Louth

D. N. Robinson (2000) Geomorphology of the Lincolnshire Wolds: An Excursion Guide, *Mercian Geologist* 15 (i), 41–48

D. N. Robinson (2007) *The Story of Hubbard's Hills.* Louth

Chapter 2

R. H. Bewley ed. (1998) *Lincolnshire's Archaeology from the Air.* Lincoln

N. Loughlin and K. R. Miller (1979) *A. Survey of Archaeological Sites in Humberside.* Hull

J. May (1976) *Prehistoric Lincolnshire.* Lincoln

P. Phillips ed. (1989) *Archaeology and Landscape Studies in North Lincolnshire.* Oxford

P. Sawyer (1998) *Anglo-Saxon Lincolnshire.* Lincoln

A. Vince ed. (1993) *Pre-Viking Lindsey.* Lincoln

J. B. Whitwell (1992) *Roman Lincolnshire.* Lincoln

An extended version of this chapter is available on the Lincolnshire County Council website: www.lincolnshire.gov.uk

Chapter 3

K. J. Allinson (1970) *Deserted Villages.* London

G. Beresford (1987) *Goltho: The Development of an Early Medieval Manor*

M. Beresford (1987) *The Lost Villages of England.* Gloucester

M. Beresford and J. G. Hurst (1989) *Deserted Medieval Villages.* Gloucester

R. Muir (1982) *The Lost Villages of Britain.* London

T. Rowley and J. Wood (1985) *Deserted Villages.* Princes Risborough

D. Start (2001) Deserted Medieval Villages in *An Historical Atlas of Lincolnshire* eds S. Bennett and N. Bennett. Chichester

Chapter 4

T. W. Beastall (1978) *The Agricultural Revolution in Lincolnshire.* Lincoln

Countryside Commission (1993) *The Lincolnshire Wolds Landscape.* Banbury

R. Olney (1979) *Rural Society and County Government in Nineteenth Century Lincolnshire.* Lincoln

M. Overton (1996) *Agricultural Revolution in England.* Cambridge

C. K. Rawding (2001) *The Lincolnshire Wolds in the Nineteenth Century.* Lincoln

A. Young (1970) *General View of Agriculture in the County of Lincoln 1813.* Newton Abbot

Chapter 5

R. C. Russell (1988) *The Enclosures of Searby 1763–65, Nettleton 1791–95 and Caistor Moors 1811–14*. Nettleton

E. and R. C. Russell (1983) *Making New Landscapes in Lincolnshire*. Lincoln

E. and R. C. Russell (1985) *Old and New Landscapes in the Horncastle Area*. Lincoln

E. and R. C. Russell (1987) *Parliamentary Enclosure and New Lincolnshire Landscapes*. Lincoln

Chapter 6

S. Bennett and N. Bennett (2001) *An Historical Atlas of Lincolnshire*. Chichester

J. Boyes and R. Russell (1977) *The Canals of Eastern England* (1977)

G. Dow (1959) *Great Central*

A. J. Ludlam and W. B. Herbert (1987) *The Louth to Bardney Branch*. Headington

D. R. Mills ed. (1989) *Twentieth Century Lincolnshire*. Lincoln

S. M. Sizer and J. Clark (2006) *People and Boats: A. History of Louth Canal*. Louth

S. E. Squires (1988) *The Lost Railways of Lincolnshire*. Lincoln

N. R. Wright (1982) *Lincolnshire Towns and Industry 1700–1914*. Lincoln

J. Wrottesley (1979) *The Great Northern Railway*. Lincoln

Chapter 7

N. Pevsner and J. Harris, revised N. Antram (1989) *The Buildings of Lincolnshire*. London

D. N. Robinson (1999) *Lincolnshire Bricks: History and Gazetteer*. Heckington

H. H. Swinnerton and P.E. Kent (1981) *The Geology of Lincolnshire*. Lincoln

Chapter 8

R. Blake, M. Hodgson and W. Taylor (1984) *Airfields of Lincolnshire since 1912*. Hinckley

M. Bragg, RDF: *The Location of Aircraft by Radio Methods* (2001)

S. Finn (1989) *The Black Swan* (Elsham Wolds)

T. N. Hancock (2004) *Bomber County: A. History of the RAF in Lincolnshire*. Hinckley

P. Otter (1990) *Lincolnshire Airfields in the Second World War*. Reading

P. Otter (1991) *Maximum Effort: The Story of the North Lincolnshire Bombers*

P. Otter (1991) *Maximum Effort 2: One Group at War*. Cherry Burton

P. Otter (1993) *Maximum Effort 3: The Untold Stories*. Cherry Burton

C. S. Parker (1991) *The Royal Observer Corps in Lincolnshire 1936–1991*

S. Scott and J. Jackson (1990) *Attack to Defence: The History of RAF Binbrook*

J. Wright (1996) *On Wings of War: 164 Squadron*

Chapter 9

A. S. Byatt (1990) *Possession*

J. Lord ed. (2007) *Peter DeWint 1784–1849 'For the Common Observer of Life and Nature'*. Aldershot

A. Roberts ed. (2000) *Alfred Tennyson*. Oxford

D. Robinson and C. Sturman (2001) *William Brown and the Louth Panorama*. Louth

J. and P. Roworth (2006) *Lincolnshire Moods*. Tiverton

A. Wheatcroft (1980) *The Tennyson Album*. London

Chapter 10
J. Brown (2005) *Farming in Lincolnshire 1850–1945*. Lincoln
D. R. Mills ed. (1989) *Twentieth Century Lincolnshire*. Lincoln
R. J. Olney (1975) *Labouring Life on the Lincolnshire Wolds*. Sleaford

Chapter 11
Lincolnshire Biodiversity Action Plan 2nd ed. (2006) Horncastle
A. E. Smith (1996) *Nature in Lincolnshire: Towards a Biodiversity Strategy*. Horncastle
A. E. Smith (2007) *Trustees for Nature: A Memoir*. Horncastle
G. Trinder (2008) *Wild Lincolnshire*. Horncastle

Chapter 12
H. Marrows (2007) *Walking in the Wolds*. Horncastle

Chapter 13
R. Woolmore (2006) *Lincolnshire Wolds AONB – Designation History Series*

Chapter 14
E. Holdaway and G. Smart (2001) *Landscape at Risk? The future of Areas of Outstanding Natural Beauty*
The Lincolnshire Wolds Interpretation Strategy (2001) Lincoln
The Lincolnshire Wolds Landscape Assessment (1993)
The Lincolnshire Wolds AONB Management Plan 2004–2009 (2004) Louth

Useful websites:
www.lincswolds.org.uk
www.aonb.org.uk
www.visitaonb.org.uk

Vignettes
D. N. Robinson (2007) *The Story of Hubbard's Hills*. Louth
A. Ward (1996) *The Lincolnshire Rising 1536*. Louth
B. Brammer (1994) *Winceby and the Battle*. Boston
D. Kaye, S. Scorer and D. N. Robinson (1992) *Fowler of Louth*. Louth
The Poems of Henry Winn. (1965) Nettleton
D. N. Robinson (2000) *The Louth Flood 29 May 1920*. Louth

Index

Numbers in italics refer to figures.